Editor in Chief
Ina Massler Levin, M.A.

Creative Director
Karen Goldfluss, M.S. Ed.

Illustrator
Clint McKnight

Cover Artist
Barb Lorseyedi

Art Coordinator
Renée Christine Yates

Imaging
Leonard P. Swierski

Publisher

Mary D. Smith, M.S. Ed.

Nonfiction & Fiction Reading Comprehension

GRADE 5

Practice Makes Perfect

Contributing Authors
Ruth Foster, M. Ed.
Eric Migliaccio

Teacher Created Resources, Inc.
6421 Industry Way
Westminster, CA 92683
www.teachercreated.com

ISBN: 978-1-4206-3046-6

© 2010 Teacher Created Resources, Inc.
Made in U.S.A.

Teacher Created Resources

Table of Contents

Introduction

The old adage "practice makes perfect" can really hold true for your child and his or her education. The more practice and exposure your child has with concepts being taught in school, the more success he or she is likely to find. For many parents, knowing how to help their children may be frustrating because the resources may not be readily available.

As a parent, it is also difficult to know where to focus your efforts so that the extra practice your child receives at home supports what he or she is learning in school.

This book has been written to help parents and teachers reinforce basic skills with children. *Practice Makes Perfect: Nonfiction & Fiction Reading Comprehension* gives children practice with reading and answering questions that help them fully comprehend what they have read. The inclusion of both a nonfiction article and a fictional story for each set of questions gives children practice with reading, comparing, and contrasting two related—but fundamentally different—written pieces.

The exercises in this book can be done sequentially or can be taken out of order, as needed. After reading the stories, children will answer most of the questions by filling in bubbles on the question pages. This gives them practice with answering questions in the format of many standardized tests.

The following standards or objectives will be met or reinforced by completing the practice pages included in this book. These standards or objectives are similar to the ones required by your state and school district and are appropriate for fifth grade:

- The student will demonstrate competence in using various skills and strategies to read the stories and answer the questions.

- The student will demonstrate competence in plot, setting, themes, and other literary elements.

- The student will demonstrate competence in finding the story's main idea, making inferences, and making predictions.

How to Make the Most of This Book

Here are some useful ideas for making the most of this book:

- Set aside a specific place in your home to work on this book. Keep the area neat, tidy, and stocked with needed materials.

- Establish consistency by setting up a certain time of day to work on these practice pages.

- Keep all practice sessions with your child positive and constructive.

- Read aloud with your child and participate by asking the comprehension questions.

- Review the work your child has done. Pay attention to the areas in which your child has the most difficulty. Provide extra guidance and exercises in those areas.

Nonfiction

An Optical Illusion

An optical illusion is not real. It is something your eyes see even though it's not really there. For instance, there is a trick you can do that will make you see a hole in your hand. The hole is not really there. The hole is an optical illusion.

To do this trick, all you need is a tube from a paper-towel roll. Take the tube and hold it up to one eye. Keep both eyes open and look at an object in the distance through the tube. Next, place one hand on one side of the tube. Keep focusing on the distant object. Soon, there will appear to be a hole in the hand that is resting against the tube!

What makes this trick work? Your field of vision involves two eyes. Your brain receives information from both eyes, and your brain merges this information.

When you look through the tube, your brain gets confused. This is because your field of vision is not the same for both eyes. One eye is looking at something close (your hand), while the other eye is focusing on an object far away. Your brain takes the two images and superimposes them. It layers one image over the over. When the images are superimposed, it appears that you have a hole in your hand.

Fiction

Kimiko's Thumb

Kimiko said, "Mr. Patterson, you are big, and I am small. Still, all I need is my thumb to stop you from standing up!"

As Mr. Patterson stopped the class from laughing, he said, "Would you like to show us how it is possible?"

Nodding, Kimiko went to the front of the class. She asked Mr. Patterson to sit all the way back in his chair with his hands on his lap. Once Mr. Patterson followed her instructions, Kimiko put her thumb in the middle of Mr. Patterson's forehead. "Try to stand up without using your hands or arms to help," she said.

As Mr. Patterson tried to stand up, Kimiko pushed on Mr. Patterson's forehead with her thumb. Mr. Patterson was a lot bigger than Kimiko, but he could not stand up!

"How is that possible?" asked Jack.

Mr. Patterson explained, "Everything has a center of gravity or center of mass. Our center of mass is where most of our mass is concentrated. For people, if our center of mass is not over our base of support, we fall over. If we are sitting, our base of support is a chair. If we are standing, our base of support is our feet. In this case, I could not stand up from a seated position because I needed to lean forward to move my center of mass over my feet. Kimiko's mighty thumb stopped me from leaning forward."

Directions: Fill in the bubble next to each correct answer.

1. **When two images are superimposed, they are**

   Ⓐ placed side by side.

   Ⓑ merged with both eyes.

   Ⓒ called our field of vision.

   Ⓓ layered one over the other.

2. **You can tell that at first no one thought Kimiko could keep Mr. Patterson from standing up because everyone**

   Ⓐ needed to lean forward.

   Ⓑ asked how it was possible.

   Ⓒ followed her instructions.

   Ⓓ laughed at what she had said.

3. **Mr. Patterson would most likely agree with which statement?**

   Ⓐ Kimiko has the only mighty thumb.

   Ⓑ Kimiko's center of gravity is not in her thumb.

   Ⓒ Kimiko's thumb stopped his brain from getting information.

   Ⓓ Kimiko made an optical illusion when he tried to stand up.

4. **Look at the picture to the right. Which story does it show?**

   Ⓐ "An Optical Illusion"

   Ⓑ "Kimiko's Thumb"

5. **Should you judge something by how it looks? Write one or more paragraphs telling why you should or should not. Use information from the stories in your answer.**

   _____

   _____

   _____

   _____

Nonfiction

The Big Discovery

When most people think of rodents, they think of rats or mice. They think of small things with big front teeth. But not all rodents are small. In fact, scientists have just discovered the remains of a very large rodent.

Exactly how big was this rodent? Scientists think it may have been more than 8 feet long and weighed over 2,000 pounds. In other words, think of a mouse as big as a bull!

The funny thing about this fossil is that it was discovered twice. It was found the first time in 1987 in Uruguay, a country in South America. The man who discovered the fossil gave it to a museum. The fossil sat in a box, hidden from view in the museum, until it was rediscovered more than 20 years later when the box was finally opened.

Scientists could tell that the animal was a rodent because of the shape of its skull and its huge incisors. Incisors are front teeth with a cutting edge. Scientists could tell from the teeth that the animal was an herbivore, or plant-eater.

Scientists think that the rodent lived in lowland rain forests between two and four million years ago. Scientists think it may have used its huge incisors to protect itself. They may have been used to ward off saber-toothed cats or giant, flightless, meat-eating birds.

Fiction

Which Pet to Get?

Mandy said, "Dad, can I please have a pet? A feline or a canine would be best. I promise that I'll behave responsibly and take care of it."

Mandy's father replied, "I don't want you to get a feline or a canine. A cat would jump onto counters, sit on the furniture, and leave its hair everywhere. A dog would bark and would have to be taken out for walks. No, you cannot have a feline or a canine."

Mandy said, "How about if I have a reptile for a pet? I could have a snake! A snake would not leave hair anywhere, and it would not bark."

Her father answered, "Snakes are reptiles, and they are carnivores. They eat meat. You would have to feed your snake live mice. No, you cannot have a snake."

Mandy said, "Mice are rodents. Could I have a rodent? I could take good care of a rodent."

Mandy's father thought about mice, guinea pigs, and rats. They are all small. "All right," he agreed.

When Mandy's father came home the next day, he stared in shock at Mandy's pet. It wasn't small! It was a rodent the size of a small pig!

Mandy grinned as she said, "Isn't my capybara the greatest, Dad?" The capybara is the world's largest rodent. It comes from South America. It can weigh up to 143 pounds!

Directions: Fill in the bubble next to each correct answer.

1. **What is most likely not true about the largest rodent that ever lived?**

   Ⓐ It ate meat.

   Ⓑ It was a big as a bull.

   Ⓒ It had huge front teeth.

   Ⓓ It lived between two and four million years ago.

2. **Most likely, Mandy's capybara**

   Ⓐ ate live mice.   Ⓒ had large incisors.

   Ⓑ did not have hair.   Ⓓ was discovered in 1987.

3. **From the stories, one can tell that a saber-toothed tiger is**

   Ⓐ a canine carnivore.   Ⓒ a canine herbivore.

   Ⓑ a feline carnivore.   Ⓓ a feline herbivore.

4. **Keep them straight! Write down one example of each.**

feline	canine	reptile	rodent

5. **Circle the teeth you think are the incisors. Copy down the sentence or sentences you read in the story that helped you pick your answer.**

Pockets Full of Evidence

In 1923, a gang attempted to rob a train in southern Oregon. Only one thing was left at the scene of the crime: a pair of greasy overalls. The police didn't know who had committed the crime. Hoping the overalls could help solve the case, the police sent them to a forensic scientist.

A forensic scientist looks for evidence that is hard fact and can be used in a court of law. The evidence does not come from a witness. It is not what someone saw happen.

The forensic scientist told the police that the suspect was likely a left-handed lumberjack. Why? The overall pockets on the left-hand side were more worn out than those on the right. The grease in the overalls was actually sap, and the sap came from trees being logged in southern Oregon.

The forensic scientist told the police the suspect's height, weight, hair color, and age. His evidence was the size of the overalls and a hair stuck to a button. The scientist also found bits of tobacco in the pockets and nail clippings stuck in the seams.

Lastly, the forensic scientist gave the police an address! How? The scientist had found a paper faded by washing in the overalls. By treating it with iodine, the scientist had been able to make out the words. It was a postal receipt with an address printed on it!

The Three Cases

Ms. Clancy said, "Class, yesterday we learned how forensic scientists help police solve cases. Today, I am going to give you some cases to solve. You don't need forensic evidence to discover a solution, but you'll need to listen carefully."

"The first case," said Ms. Clancy, "is about a cowboy. The cowboy went into town on Friday. He stayed three days. When he left, he left on Friday. How is this possible?"

"The second case," continued Ms. Clancy, "is about a woman who married 15 men! None of the men have died, so the woman is not a widow. She has never gotten divorced, and yet this woman has never broken the law! How is this possible?"

"The third case," said Ms. Clancy, "is about a man who tumbled out of a window of a 40-story building when it was raining outside. The man was not harmed, and not a hair on his head got wet. How is this possible?"

Chase said, "I know the answer to the first case! I know how a cowboy could arrive on Friday, stay three days, and leave on Friday. His horse is named Friday!"

Ana said, "I can answer to the second one! The woman was a judge. She wasn't married to the men, but she was responsible for marrying each man to each man's own wife!"

Hannah said, "I think I can solve the third case! It's possible if it was a bald man who tumbled out of a first-floor window of a 40-story building!"

"Cases solved!" cried Ms. Clancy.

Directions: Fill in the bubble next to each correct answer.

1. From the stories, you can tell that

   Ⓐ people who are bald cannot get wet.

   Ⓑ different trees have different saps.

   Ⓒ forensic scientists solve all crimes.

   Ⓓ witnesses are not used in a court of law.

2. A widow is a woman

   Ⓐ who is a judge.   Ⓒ whose husband has died.

   Ⓑ who was never married.   Ⓓ who has married 15 men.

3. What is not forensic evidence?

   Ⓐ a track left by the cowboy's horse

   Ⓑ a receipt for the cowboy's hotel bill

   Ⓒ someone saying they saw the cowboy leave

   Ⓓ a fingerprint left by the cowboy on a glass

4. Write the letter on the line to match the evidence to what it told in the story "Pockets Full of Evidence."

   _____ sap   **a.** old address

   _____ size of overalls   **b.** left-handed

   _____ pockets   **c.** came from Oregon

   _____ receipt   **d.** height and weight

5. Look at the picture to the right. Which story does it show?

   Ⓐ "Pockets Full of Evidence"

   Ⓑ "The Three Cases"

Nonfiction

Fastest on Land

Game parks are huge areas of land where tourists can watch wild animals roam in their natural habitat. Game parks differ from zoos in that the animals are not kept in cages. Many tourists travel to the East African country of Kenya to visit the country's game parks. If a tourist is lucky, he or she may see the fastest animal on land: the cheetah.

With their long legs and slender bodies, cheetahs can reach speeds of up to 70 miles (113 km) per hour. No other animal can accelerate as fast as a cheetah. A cheetah can build its speed up to 45 miles per hour (72 km/h) from a standing start in just two seconds!

A cheetah has long claws that are always pushed out. This helps the cheetah to accelerate. The claws work the same way cleats on track shoes do. They dig into the ground, keeping the cheetah from slipping as it pushes off. No other cat, big or small, has claws that are permanently pushed out.

Cheetahs are spotted, but they do have two black stripes on their bodies. The stripes, called "tear lines," are on a cheetah's face and run from its eyes to its mouth. Tear lines may not help a cheetah run fast, but they do help protect a cheetah's eyes from the glare of the sun.

Fiction

A Kenyan Folk Tale

Long, long ago, Vulture sailed through the skies. "I consume the flesh of lions and other dangerous predators," bragged Vulture. "I am Master of the Wind!" Down below, Chameleon perched on the limb of a large acacia tree and opened one eye. Vulture's bragging had woken him up.

"Bragging, bragging, bragging," Chameleon said in disgust. "Vulture, you're constantly bragging. You should stop your racket and let me sleep."

Vulture landed close to Chameleon. Vulture couldn't see Chameleon because Chameleon was the same color as the acacia tree. "Chameleon," Vulture said, "Show yourself so we can race. Let us race to the river. You'll have to crawl, but I'll fly. You who can hide will see that I'm far better than you, for I'll easily be the victor. Yes, you'll see that I am the true Master!"

Chameleon agreed to the race. Even before the race started, Vulture began to brag about winning. Vulture was so busy making a racket that he didn't notice Chameleon grabbing onto his tail. Chameleon held tightly onto Vulture's tail as Vulture began to soar through the air. Chameleon was so light that Vulture did not know he was there.

Vulture flew to the river. "Yes," said Vulture. "I am Master of the Wind! I don't see Chameleon anywhere. I've won the race." But as Vulture flapped his wings to land, he heard a little voice. It was right below him.

"Watch where you land!" cried out Chameleon. "I've been waiting for you. Don't sit on me!"

Directions: Fill in the bubble next to each correct answer.

1. **What do both stories have in common?**

   Ⓐ They both are about animals in a race.

   Ⓑ They both are about animals with spots.

   Ⓒ They both are about animals found in Kenya.

   Ⓓ They both are about animals that make a racket.

2. **From the stories, you can tell that**

   Ⓐ a vulture can go faster than a cheetah.

   Ⓑ a cheetah can go faster than a vulture.

   Ⓒ a chameleon can go faster than a cheetah.

   Ⓓ a cheetah can go faster than a chameleon.

3. **Baseball players sometimes put black grease under their eyes. Most likely, the grease acts the same way as a**

   Ⓐ vulture's wings.   Ⓒ chameleon's color.

   Ⓑ cheetah's spots.   Ⓓ cheetah's tear lines.

4. **Circle the foot and face that most likely belongs to a cheetah. Tell how you know.**

   _____

   _____

5. **Give some reasons why a game park might be better than a zoo. Then, give some reasons why a zoo might be better than a game park.**

   _____

   _____

   _____

   _____

Nonfiction

An Innate Fear

Scientists performed an experiment with two-day old chicks. For the experiment, each chick was tested one at a time. Different V-shaped shadows were moved over the chicks. The point of the V was pointed in different directions. Sometimes it was pointed like this: <. Other times it was pointed like this: >.

The chicks responded differently to each shadow. If the shadow was moved open-end first over the chicks, the chicks were not scared. They did not show fear. If, though, the shadow was turned around so that the point-end led the way, the chicks responded fearfully.

Scientists believe that the response of the chicks shows that some animals have built-in or innate fears. When it moves to the right, a shadow like this < matches a silhouette of a flying duck. A silhouette is a dark shape seen against a light background. Chicks have no reason to fear the silhouette of a flying duck.

A shadow shaped like this > has a different silhouette when it moves to the right. It matches the silhouette of a flying hawk. Hawks are birds of prey, and their diet consists of small animals. To a hawk, a small chick would be a tasty meal.

A chick's innate fear makes it so the chick is more likely to grow up, as the chick doesn't have to be attacked to learn that hawks are dangerous. The chick is innately programmed to know that the hawk's shape means danger.

Fiction

Fears and Phobias

Ms. Walters said, "Class, today I'm going to give you a fun quiz on phobias. A phobia is a fear so strong that it isn't normal. Suppose I were dreadfully afraid of animals. Do you think I would have claustrophobia or zoophobia?"

Chang said, "I know that zoos are filled with animals, so I'm going to guess you have zoophobia."

Ms. Walters said, "Chang, you're absolutely right! If someone has zoophobia, they have a dreadful fear of animals. If someone has claustrophobia, they have a dreadful fear of closed-in spaces. Closed-in places make them feel like they are trapped."

"Okay," said Ms. Walters, "I am afraid of mice. I see a mouse, and I scream! I can't stand mice! Do I have musophobia or hydrophobia?"

Davis said, "I do not know what hydrophobia means, but it makes me think of fire hydrants. It does not make me think of mice. Do you have musophobia?"

"Very good," said Ms. Walters. "Musophobia is the fear of mice. Hydrophobia is the fear of water."

All of a sudden Eva said, "Ms. Walters, I hope you don't have arachnophobia!"

"Why is that?" asked Ms. Walters, with a smile on her face.

"Because," said Eva, "the big hairy spider I brought to show the class isn't where I left it in my desk!"

Directions: Fill in the bubble next to each correct answer.

1. **When moving to the right, a shadow like this < looks like the silhouette of a**

   (A) hawk.

   (B) duck.

   (C) chick.

   (D) shadow.

2. **Most likely, arachnophobia is the fear of**

   (A) zoos.

   (B) water.

   (C) spiders.

   (D) elevators.

3. **Most likely, a scientist would not call a chick's fear of a hawk's shadow a phobia because**

   (A) it is a normal fear for a chick.

   (B) it is a fear that the chick learns.

   (C) chicks are not afraid of all shadows.

   (D) the chicks were part of an experiment.

4. **Look at the picture to the right. This man might be very uncomfortable in this situation if he suffered from**

   (A) musophobia.

   (B) hydrophobia.

   (C) claustrophobia.

   (D) arachnophobia.

5. **Choose one of the phobias in the story "Fears and Phobias." Tell what the life of someone with that phobia might be like. Tell what you might do to help someone overcome that phobia.**

_____

_____

_____

_____

Safe and Warm

Wendy Murphy was watching the news. The year was 1985, and a terrible earthquake had hit Mexico City, Mexico. A hospital had collapsed. Wendy watched as rescue workers struggled to carry babies out of the rubble. The tiny babies had been sleeping in the hospital's incubators. Incubators are heated cribs that are used to keep babies warm.

Wendy saw the babies being carried on stretchers. The stretchers were too big and not suitable for the tiny babies. Workers had to hold the babies down onto the stretchers to keep them from falling off. This made it harder to move and more difficult to go fast. Watching the terrible scene, Wendy thought, "There has to be a better way."

Wendy worked at a hospital for sick children. Wendy started thinking about a stretcher that would be just for babies. She made sketches of a stretcher with three pockets. Each pocket could hold two babies. The babies could not fall out of the pockets.

When Wendy designed her stretcher, she looked at all types of fabrics. She finally chose a heavy silver material. What was this heavy silver material used for? It was used in pizza delivery bags! It was used to keep pizzas warm!

Today, Wendy's stretchers are used all around the world. Thanks to Wendy's invention, babies can be rescued quickly. Babies can be moved safely and kept warm, too!

The History of the X-Ray

One day, Miguel fell off his bike and hurt his arm. When Miguel went to the hospital, the doctor took an x-ray, or picture, of Miguel's bone. The x-ray showed that Miguel's arm was fractured, or broken. As the doctor put Miguel's arm in a cast, Miguel asked, "Who invented the x-ray?"

The doctor smiled at Miguel. He said, "A man named William Roentgen took the first x-ray on December 22, 1895. He took a picture of his wife's hand. She was not happy about it!"

"But it's just an x-ray," said Miguel. "It doesn't hurt."

"Yes, but she thought looking at her bones was like seeing herself already dead! People were afraid of x-rays at first," the doctor continued. "They were afraid because x-rays could 'see' through clothes. One company in England started selling special underclothes! The company claimed that their underclothes were x-ray proof!"

As the doctor finished putting on Miguel's cast, he said, "You have something in common with the first x-ray taken in the United States. That x-ray was taken on February 3, 1896. A doctor brought his patient into a laboratory in New Hampshire. The x-ray showed that the patient's arm was fractured in the same place that your arm is broken!"

Laughing, Miguel said, "Wow. Do you think the patient fell off his bike, too?"

Directions: Fill in the bubble next to each correct answer.

1. Both stories are about

    (A) inventions from the 1800s.

    (B) inventions that help doctors.

    (C) inventions used to show fractures.

    (D) inventions first made to help babies.

2. Using Wendy's stretcher, how many babies could rescuers carry at once?

    (A) 2

    (B) 4

    (C) 6

    (D) 8

3. From "The History of the X-Ray," you can tell that Roentgen

    (A) did not take the first x-ray in Canada.

    (B) did not take the first x-ray in Mexico.

    (C) did not take the first x-ray in England.

    (D) did not take the first x-ray in the United States.

4. Fill in the chart to show how different people felt or might feel about x-rays.

Roentgen's wife	People in 1895	Miguel's doctor	Miguel

5. Look at the picture to the right. Which story does it show?

    (A) "Safe and Warm"

    (B) "The History of the X-Ray"

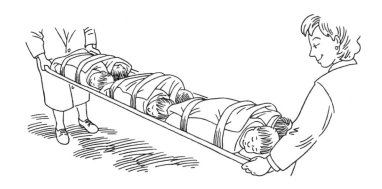

What Was for Dinner

David Love was a geologist who studied rocks, fossils, and the Earth's crust. He grew up in Wyoming on a ranch in the early 1900s. When David was born, he and his brother were the only children within a thousand square miles (2,590 sq. km).

Once, when David and his brother were young, they killed a huge rattlesnake. To David's family, the snake was more than a dangerous and poisonous viper: it was food. That night, David's mother served the snake for dinner. She served it creamed on toast.

There was a guest for dinner the night the rattlesnake was served. David's father told David and his brother that they were not to use the word "rattlesnake" at the table. Instead, the boys were to use the word "chicken." This was, their father said, because the guest might not be too happy about eating a poisonous viper.

During the meal, David and his brother started talking about rattlesnakes and other poisonous vipers. They talked about how often they encountered snakes and where the vipers' dens could be found. They also said how very good rattlesnakes were to eat.

Their guest responded, "If anybody ever gave me rattlesnake meat, I'd kill them."

David and his brother became very quiet, but their mother simply asked the guest if he wanted more chicken.

"Don't mind if I do," the guest replied.

Eating a Dinosaur

Alejandro said, "You said I could have what I wanted, and I told you that I don't want to eat anything but a dinosaur on my birthday!"

Alejandro's mother sighed. She said, "Alejandro, be reasonable. How can I get you a dinosaur to eat? Dinosaurs are extinct. They died out a long time ago."

Angrily, Alejandro said, "Then I won't be eating anything on my birthday!"

As Alejandro's birthday got closer and closer, everyone began to tease him. They said things like, "Better fill up now because you won't be eating anything on your birthday!"

Alejandro's big brother Thomas told his mother he would find a dinosaur for Alejandro to eat. "You know dinosaurs are extinct," his mother replied tiredly.

All of Alejandro's friends came over on his birthday. They cried, "We've come for dinosaur! Alejandro said we could eat some dinosaur on his birthday!"

Alejandro's mother started to explain that dinosaurs were extinct, but then Thomas came in. He was carrying a dinosaur! The dinosaur had big brown spikes down its back. It had sharp yellow teeth, and its skin was covered with green and black spots.

Grinning, Thomas said, "I made a cake in the shape of a circle. Then I cut it up and arranged it into a dinosaur shape. I decorated it with chocolate, candy corn, and gumdrops."

Everyone agreed that Thomas's cake was the best-tasting dinosaur they had ever had!

16

Directions: Fill in the bubble next to each correct answer.

1. **When a type of animal is no longer living, it is**

   Ⓐ reasonable.

   Ⓒ decorated.

   Ⓑ arranged.

   Ⓓ extinct.

2. **What do both stories have in common?**

   Ⓐ animals that have become extinct

   Ⓑ sharing food with birthday guests

   Ⓒ encountering snakes and other vipers

   Ⓓ eating something one would not expect to

3. **From the stories, you can tell that most likely some**

   Ⓐ snakes taste like cake.

   Ⓒ snakes taste like chicken.

   Ⓑ dinosaurs taste like cake.

   Ⓓ dinosaurs taste like chicken.

4. **List in order what happens in the story. Use the numbers 1 to 5. Put "1" by what happened first. Put "5" by what happened last.**

   _____ David and his brother talk about where to find snake dens.

   _____ David's mother offers more chicken to their guest.

   _____ David and his brother are told not to use the word "rattlesnake."

   _____ David and his brother kill a rattlesnake.

   _____ The guest says he would kill anyone who serves him rattlesnake.

5. **Look at the labeled pictures. One shows the round cake when Thomas first cut it, and the other shows the cake after Thomas arranged it into the shape of a dinosaur. Some of the labels are missing on the dinosaur cake. Which labels should be on the following dinosaur parts:**

   body _____

   tail _____

   top of the head _____

Willie's Catch

In the eighth inning of the 1954 World Series, the score was tied 2–2. The New York Giants were in the field, and the Cleveland Indians were at bat. Two Indians were already on base, when the Indians' Vic Wertz hit a fly ball deep into center field. As it soared through the air, no one thought the ball could be caught. It seemed to be going too far too fast. The Indians were going to score and win the game.

One man sprang into action. Turning his back on the infield, the centerfielder ran toward the outfield fence as fast as he could. He ran toward deep center field—nearly 440 feet (134 meters) from home plate—before he took a quick glance back, raised his mitt, and caught the ball as it was flying over his shoulder!

As soon as he had caught the ball, the man spun around and threw the ball into the infield. His actions were so quick that the runners on base never had a chance to score! The Giants won the World Series that year. Many people say it was due to the play now known simply as "The Catch."

The player who made this impossible catch was Willie Mays. Willie played baseball for 22 seasons and is considered one of the greatest players of all time. But in the first six games of his career, he got only 1 hit in 26 times at bat! Good thing he didn't give up because by the end of his career, Willie had a total of 3,283 hits. He also scored 2,062 runs and hit 660 home runs.

A Winning Attitude

Mr. Martz said, "Class, why does it take longer to run from second base to third base than it takes to run from first base to second base?"

Mr. Martz's eyes twinkled as he looked at his students. "Don't look so worried," he said. "It's a joke! The answer is, 'Because there's a short stop between second and third.'"

After the class stopped laughing, Mr. Martz said, "I wanted you to laugh, because being in a good humor fits the person I'll be discussing. Willie Mays was a baseball player whose nickname was 'The Say Hey Kid.' Willie's nickname came about because Willie always greeted his teammates with a friendly 'Say hey.' Willie was a skillful player, but there was something extra he added to a baseball team. He made it fun to play, and his pleasure in participating rubbed off on other players. In fact, one manager from an opposing team once said how Willie could help a team. He did not mention Willie's hitting, running, or throwing skills. Instead, he mentioned Willie's attitude. He said Willie could help a team 'just by riding on the bus with them.'"

Directions: Fill in the bubble next to each correct answer.

1. **Willie Mays made "The Catch" when he was running**

   (A) in the infield with his back to the infield.

   (B) in the infield with his back to the outfield.

   (C) in the outfield with his back to the infield.

   (D) in the outfield with his back to the outfield.

2. **When one participates, one**

   (A) is in a good humor. (C) takes part with others.

   (B) has a good attitude. (D) finds pleasure in a joke.

3. **Most likely, if Willie had not made "The Catch," he would have**

   (A) wished he had never played baseball.

   (B) tried even harder the rest of the game.

   (C) said the ball was impossible to catch.

   (D) gotten angry at the player who hit the ball.

4. **Fill in the circle next to the player that shows the position Willie Mays was in when he made "An Impossible Catch."**

   (A)   (B)

5. **Do you think one person's attitude can change how other people feel? Explain your answer. You may choose to use an example to support your answer.**

   _____

   _____

   _____

   _____

A Corps Member

The explorers were hungry. To survive, the explorers would have to trade with the Nez Perce for food. Who was the man sent to do the trading with the Native Americans? Who was the man who traded brass buttons cut off of military uniforms for three bushels of edible roots and some bread made of lily roots?

The trader was a slave named York. York was part of the Lewis and Clark expedition called the Corps of Discovery. The expedition began in 1804 and ended in 1806. The Corps's purpose was to explore the unmapped west. It started out in St. Louis, Missouri, and journeyed all the way to the Pacific Ocean and back.

York was Clark's slave. Clark told York he needed him because he knew York could help. York was strong and a good hunter. He was the only slave on the expedition.

York could not read or write. He could not record what he saw or felt. We know what York did because of what other men wrote in their journals. In a journal entry, Clark recorded how York swam to a sandbar in the middle of a river to gather greens for dinner. The explorer's diet was mostly meat, so York's greens were a real treat.

The Only Woman

My name is Sacagawea, and I am a Shoshone Native American. I am also the only woman who went with Lewis and Clark on their expedition to the Pacific Ocean. Often, as the men paddled their boats, I would walk along the shore. One time, a huge gust of wind sprang up, causing one of the boats to tip on its side. Men shouted and yelled as the boat's cargo slid into the water.

I wasn't sure what some of the cargo was for, but I knew it was precious to Lewis and Clark. As the desperate men tried to right the boat, I quickly jumped into the water and began to collect the items that were beginning to float away. I saved medicines and strange-looking objects that the men looked through and at. I saved papers that the men made marks in every day.

There was one man on the expedition who looked like no other man I'd ever seen. His name was York, and his skin was black. York was very strong and a very good hunter. He took good care of Clark. He even searched Clark's blankets for fleas every day when we camped near the ocean!

The people we met were not scared of me because I was a woman with a child. They also liked York. They thought he was a great warrior.

Directions: Fill in the bubble next to each correct answer.

1. **What are both stories about?**

   Ⓐ people who were part of the Corps of Discovery

   Ⓑ the only black people in the Corps of Discovery

   Ⓒ the most powerful people in the Corps of Discovery

   Ⓓ all the people in the Corps of Discovery who could swim

2. **York traded brass military buttons for**

   Ⓐ bread made out of oak roots.

   Ⓑ bread made out of pine roots.

   Ⓒ bread made out of lily roots.

   Ⓓ bread made out of green roots.

3. **When Sacagawea jumped into the water, we do not know if she saved**

   Ⓐ papers.

   Ⓑ blankets.

   Ⓒ medicines.

   Ⓓ strange-looking objects.

4. **Fill in the boxes. Tell one way in which York and Sacagawea were the same. Tell one way in which they were different.**

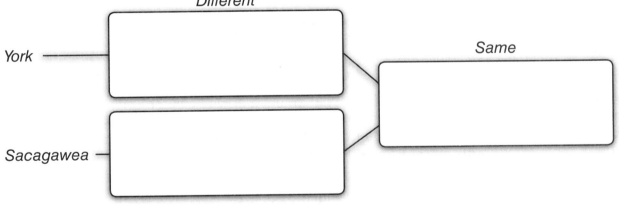

Different

York

Sacagawea

Same

5. **List two things York did on the expedition.**

   1. _____

   _____

   2. _____

   _____

Nonfiction

Seeing Through Skin

Imagine having transparent skin. If your skin were transparent, you could see through it. You would be able to see your internal organs, like your heart, lungs, and kidneys.

You may not be transparent, but there are frogs that are. Some of the frogs live high in the treetops of Central and South American rainforests. Other transparent frogs come from Japan. These frogs were developed by scientists. They were bred for their light-colored skin. The frog's skin is so light that one can see through it, and the frog's organs, veins, and arteries are completely visible.

Scientists bred these frogs for a reason. Before, scientists had to dissect, or cut open, a frog when they wanted to look at its internal workings. Scientists could learn about frogs from dissecting them, but the information they gathered was only a moment in time. It was like a snapshot. It did not show them a process.

By using transparent frogs, scientists can watch over time how organs develop. They can study the effect of toxins and tumors on organ development. A toxin is a poison. A tumor is a growth of extra tissue on some part of the body.

Transparent frogs cannot be exposed to direct light. Their skin is too light-colored to protect its internal workings from the sun. Trees protect rainforest frogs from the direct sun. In the lab, scientists are careful to only use dull light.

Fiction

Eva's New Boots

One morning Nellie said, "Please set an extra bowl, Mom. My invisible friend, Eva, is coming for breakfast."

Nellie's mother tried not to smile as she set out an extra bowl. "Good morning, Eva," she said and poured a little bit of cereal into the bowl. Then she walked over to the counter to pour herself a cup of coffee. When she turned around, she saw that the extra bowl was empty. "Eva was hungry," she said smiling. "Does she want some more?"

"No," Nellie answered, "but she wants to know if she can have your old boots."

Looking puzzled, Nellie's mother asked, "What old boots?"

"The ones you lost in the woods last summer," replied Nellie.

"Oh," said Nellie's mother. "Of course she can have them."

Just then Nellie's mother heard the door open. "That's strange," she said.

"It's just Eva leaving," said Nellie. "Mom, she's awfully glad you let her have the boots. Her feet get real cold when she has to walk barefoot in the snow."

Nellie's mother laughed. When she went to shut the door, she noticed fresh boot tracks going down the steps and across the yard towards the woods. She also noticed a different set of footprints coming the other way. The footprints were beginning to fill with snow, but they looked very much like the tracks of a barefoot child.

Directions: Fill in the bubble next to each correct answer.

1. **Which is not an organ?**

   Ⓐ lung

   Ⓑ vein

   Ⓒ heart

   Ⓓ kidney

3. **Most likely, the development of see-through frogs might mean**

   Ⓐ fewer frogs are dissected.

   Ⓑ fewer scientists study toxins.

   Ⓒ fewer frogs will develop tumors.

   Ⓓ fewer scientists will go to rain forests.

2. **A fiction story is not real. One can tell that "Eva's New Boots" is fiction because**

   Ⓐ skin can never be transparent.

   Ⓑ a transparent person would not leave footprints.

   Ⓒ there cannot be a completely transparent person.

   Ⓓ scientists have not yet bred transparent arteries.

4. **Compare the two kinds of see-through frogs in "Seeing Through Skin."**

	Frog 1	Frog 2
bred by scientists (yes/no)	no	
where found		
how protected from direct light		

5. **Look at the two sets of footprints below. Which shows the set of prints that were going away from Nellie's house and into the woods at the end of the "Eva's New Boots."**

Ⓐ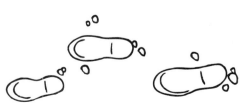

Ⓑ

Nonfiction

The Ironman

Every year, a grueling race is held in Hawaii. The race's full name is the Ironman Triathlon. This race is so tiring and exhausting that it is as if one must be made of iron to survive. The race has three parts. First, there is a 2.4-mile (4 km) swim. Second, there is a bike ride. The bike ride covers 112 miles (180 km). Lastly, there is a marathon run. This distance is a little over 26 miles (42 km).

Paula Newby-Fraser knew nothing about the Ironman Triathlon until she saw a qualifying race for it. The qualifying race was to select people to compete in the Ironman. The winners of the qualifying race would win a free trip to Hawaii. Paula wanted a free trip to Hawaii. For that reason only, she bought a bike. She had eight weeks to train for the next qualifying race.

Paula earned her free trip to Hawaii. There, she placed third in her division in the Ironman race. Paula had not trained as hard or as long as the women who beat her. Still, she had lost by only a few minutes. Paula decided to train full-time. Paula won the next Ironman in Hawaii. She went on to win a total of 21 Ironman Triathlons in Hawaii and around the world.

Fiction

A Long Race Gets Longer

Ms. Teal said, "Class, our new word of the week is 'marathon.' This is a good word to know. It means . . ."

"I know!" Tim interrupted. "It is the name of a really long race."

"Yes," said Ms. Teal. "A marathon is a race that is 26 miles and 385 yards (42.2 km) long. The race's history began in 490 BCE. This was when the Battle of Marathon took place. The battle was between the Athenians and the Persians. Legend has it that after the battle, a Greek soldier raced nonstop all the way from Marathon to Athens. After crying out, 'We are victorious,' he collapsed and died."

The students sat in stunned surprise. "You've got to be kidding us!" muttered Ralph in disbelief. "He really ran all that way and died?"

"So it is said," said Ms. Teal. "To honor this soldier, a marathon race was added to the Olympics. Its distance was about the same as the distance from Marathon to Athens."

"Now this is where ancient history gets a modern twist," continued Ms. Teal with a smile. "Today, marathons are all an exact distance of 26 miles and 385 yards (42.2 km). Why this odd measurement? The 1908 Olympics were held in London, England. The queen at that time wanted the best view of the finish. Extra distance was added on so the race would end in front of the Royal Box where the queen was sitting!"

Directions: Fill in the bubble next to each correct answer.

1. **When something is grueling,**

   (A) it is extremely difficult.   (C) it is held every year.

   (B) it is made of iron.   (D) it is a qualifying race.

2. **Paula started training for her first Ironman race**

   (A) before buying a bike.   (C) before the two women who beat her.

   (B) before going to Hawaii.   (D) before she saw the qualifying race.

3. **Most likely, the running part of the Ironman Triathlon is**

   (A) the exact distance from Marathon to Athens.

   (B) not the same distance of the 1908 Olympics.

   (C) a distance of exactly 26 miles and 385 yards (42.2 km).

   (D) the exact distance the soldier ran before he collapsed.

4. **Look at the runner to the right. Which story would he most likely be a character from.**

   (A) "The Ironman"

   (B) "A Long Race Gets Longer"

5. **Look at the pictures. For each event shown, write the distances athletes need to cover in the Ironman Triathlon.**

   _____ miles   _____ miles   _____ miles, _____ yards

   _____ kilometers   _____ kilometers   _____ kilometers

The Last of a Language

The Eyak people were fishermen who lived in Alaska. The words in their language reflected how and where they lived. For example, they had more than one word for abalone, a type of shellfish. Different kinds of abalone were called different names. They also had many different words for types of fishing nets.

The Eyak even had a word, *demexch*, for a certain thin spot of ice. This spot of ice was over a body of water and was dangerous to walk on. It was also a spot that could be a good place to squat down next to and use a line or a spear to catch a fish.

The Eyak language died on January 21, 2008. That was the day the last speaker of Eyak died. The last speaker was Marie Smith, and she was 89 years old. She had had no one to speak Eyak with for over 10 years.

When Marie was little, she had to go to a government school. At school, children were punished for speaking Eyak. Then, Marie started working in a cannery when she was very young, and she never heard the Eyak language spoken aloud there. Marie's husband did not speak Eyak, and her nine children were not interested in learning a language no one else knew.

The Code

When Joseph was in 5th grade, he had to interview his grandfather. The interview questions were for a history project. Joseph said, "Grandfather, I know you were a soldier who defended the United States in World War II. What did you do?"

Joseph's grandfather said, "I was a code-talker."

Joseph asked, "What was that?"

"There were about 400 of us," Joseph's grandfather said. "We worked in pairs. We would go into battle and pass along important information on the radio. The enemy could not understand us. They had no idea what we were saying."

"Why couldn't they understand?" asked Joseph.

"We spoke in code. The enemy was unable to break the code. And the funny thing about the code was that it was not a code to us: it was actually the Navajo language. The Navajo language is very difficult to learn, but it was the language of our mothers and fathers. It was the language I learned to speak when I was a child."

"Wow," said Joseph. "What were some of the code words?"

"Well, for some things, we substituted words. For the word 'America,' we substituted the Navajo words 'our mother.' For 'submarine,' we substituted the Navajo words 'iron fish.' For 'dive bomber,' we used the Navajo words 'sparrow hawk.' After the war, for many years, we couldn't talk about what we did. We kept a code of silence."

Directions: Fill in the bubble next to each correct answer.

1. What do both stories have in common?

(A) a language that is not understood   (C) a language that was used as a code

(B) a language that was not well known   (D) a language that is no longer spoken

2. Code talkers had to work in pairs so

(A) Navajo words could be substituted.

(B) the sent messages could be understood.

(C) no one would break the code of silence.

(D) the soldiers could learn how to speak Navajo.

3. Most likely, Marie Smith

(A) knew about different kinds of ice.

(B) was not interested in being a code talker.

(C) did not talk the last 10 years of her life.

(D) spoke Navajo when she was not speaking Eyak.

4. Fill in the boxes to match the substituted words.

(A) submarine —— [ ]

(B) dive bomber —— [ ]

(C) [ ] —— our mother

5. Think about the language you know best. Answer these questions:

• How did you learn it? _____

_____

• Do you think people will forget how to speak this language? Why or why not?

_____

_____

Cold, Dark, and Famous

Loch Ness is a massive lake in Scotland. This huge lake has deep water that is very cold and pitch black. The water is dark and murky because it is filled with dark brown particles of peat, a very soft coal. But Loch Ness isn't famous for its massive size or dark water. It's famous for Nessie, the Loch Ness Monster.

Nessie started with a legend. The legend goes that in 565 CE, an Irish monk named Saint Columba saw a man swimming in Loch Ness. Columba saw a huge beast rise up from the water. On the attack, it headed straight toward the man. Columba commanded the beast to retreat. The beast retreated, sinking back down into the murky water, and the man was saved.

Over the years, people have reported sightings of Nessie. Perhaps the most famous sighting was by R.K. Wilson. Wilson was a respected doctor who took a picture of Nessie on April 1, 1934. The photograph was published all around the world.

Years later, a man named Alastair Boyd proved that the photograph was a fake. The picture was of nothing but a toy submarine that Wilson had molded a long neck and monster head onto! Many people were angry at Boyd. They still believed the photograph was real. The funny thing is that Boyd believes Nessie is real. He is sure that in 1979 he spotted her rising out of the dark water.

Tashiki's Discovery

Tashiki Iha was excited. His family was going to Loch Ness. He said, "I want to take Nessie's picture to prove she isn't a trick. I know that she's real and not a hoax."

At Loch Ness, while Tashiki was taking a walk around the lake, he spotted a strange object sticking out of some mud close to the shore. Tashiki dug it up and showed it to his father. His father said, "Tashiki, this looks like a fossilized bone. It looks like a fossilized plesiosaur backbone!"

Tashiki was very excited because he knew that a plesiosaur was a type of dinosaur, and he knew that some people thought Nessie was a plesiosaur. Tashiki said, "Maybe Nessie really is a plesiosaur. Maybe she is the last living plesiosaur. Maybe she is like a coelacanth. The coelacanth is a fish that scientists believed was extinct and had died out 70 million years ago. Then a fisherman caught a coelacanth in 1938, proving the scientists wrong."

Tashiki and his father took the bone to a scientist. The scientist studied the bone. She said, "Yes, this is a fossilized plesiosaur bone. But it can't be Nessie. I have done tests on the bone. The tests show that this bone came from somewhere close to the ocean. Most likely, someone left it at Loch Ness for someone else to find."

Tashiki said, "Dad, I am beginning to think Nessie is a very clever hoax."

Directions: Fill in the bubble next to each correct answer.

1. **What is not true about Loch Ness?**

   (A) It is small.

   (B) Its water is cold.

   (C) It is in Scotland.

   (D) It is filled with peat.

2. **When something is a hoax, it is**

   (A) real

   (B) a bone

   (C) extinct.

   (D) a trick.

3. **It would be very hard for Tashiki to take an underwater picture of Nessie because**

   (A) the water is too cold.

   (B) the water is too murky.

   (C) the water is retreating.

   (D) the water is millions of years old.

4. **Look at the picture to the right. It shows a famous photograph taken of Nessie. Who took this famous photograph?**

   (A) Tashiki Iha

   (B) Alastair Boyd

   (C) R.K. Wilson

   (D) Tashiki's dad

5. **Think about Nessie. Do you think she could be real, or do you think she is a hoax? Explain your answer.**

   _____

   _____

   _____

   _____

Why the Mail Was Late

As Deputy Postmaster General of the American colonies from 1764 to 1775, Benjamin Franklin noticed that ships carrying mail took two weeks longer than merchant ships to cross the Atlantic Ocean. Franklin knew that merchant ships were heavier than mail ships. Heavier ships should move slower. He also knew that merchant ships had to sail down a river before leaving England, while mail ships sailed directly from the coast. Sailing a shorter distance should mean a faster crossing.

Franklin asked his cousin, who was a whaling-ship captain. His cousin said that merchant and whaling captains knew about a current. This current was like a river of water moving in the ocean. Today, we know of this current as the Gulf Stream.

Merchant ships knew to avoid the current when sailing to the colonies. Going against it slowed them down. Whaling captains knew about the current because whales often fed at its edges. Franklin's cousin said that whaling ship captains had told mail ship captains to avoid the current. The mail ship captains had not listened. Why not? Franklin's cousin said it was because the mail ship captains felt that "they were too wise" to be given advice by "simple American fishermen."

Fiction

Never Before Seen

"There is nothing we can do," the Elders said sadly. "Our village is going to be destroyed." Everyone began to cry except for one boy named Murry. People thought Murry was simple-minded. They did not think he was very smart because Murry did not care for fancy clothes or fancy things. Instead, Murry liked to be outside. He liked to spend time in the mountains looking at the wild animals he saw there.

Murry asked, "Why is the village going to be destroyed?"

"A giant said that our village would be destroyed unless we could show him something that hasn't been seen," answered one of the Elders. "That is impossible, as we have to see something in order to find it and give it to him! Now stop pestering us with your stupid questions and start packing."

Murry turned around and ran. "What a useless boy," muttered an Elder as he watched Murry begin to climb a tree. "Only a simpleton would climb trees at a time like this. Any advice he has for us wise men is useless."

Murry returned quickly and carefully handed a tiny object to the confused Elder. Murry explained. "I've followed two robins as they built their nest and laid their eggs. I know this egg is about to hatch. Give it to the giant. He will see something no one has ever seen before: he can see the hatchling as it comes out of the egg."

Directions: Fill in the bubble next to each correct answer.

1. **What is not true about the Gulf Stream?**

   (A) Whales fed at its edges.

   (C) It flows away from England.

   (B) It is a current of water.

   (D) It is like a river in the ocean.

2. **The Elders thought they could not find anything new because they**

   (A) had started packing.

   (C) knew Murry's advice was useless.

   (B) did not know robins laid eggs.

   (D) thought they had to see it to find it.

3. **Most likely, when Ben was Deputy Postmaster General,**

   (A) few, if any, letters were sent to England.

   (B) few, if any, people looked at wild animals.

   (C) few, if any, children pestered their elders.

   (D) few, if any, charts were marked with ocean currents.

4. **Think about how people thought about Murry and what he did at different parts of the story. Very briefly, jot down some of the details.**

Beginning	Middle	End

5. **Should we judge others by what they wear or do? Tell why or why not. Use an example from the stories in your answer.**

   _____

   _____

   _____

   _____

Alone in the Atlantic

Steven Callahan was in his life raft. His boat had sunk on February 4, 1982. Now he was adrift at sea and all alone somewhere in the vast expanse of the Atlantic Ocean. Without a radio and with only a few supplies, his only goal was to stay alive until he could be rescued.

Wham! Something crashed into the tiny raft, hurling it across the water. It was a huge shark! Although Steven was terrified, he took instant action. He knew that the shark could easily destroy the life raft. His life depended on his ability to scare it away. Steven stabbed at the shark with his spear gun. The shark was too big and tough to hurt, but Steven was able to annoy it enough that it swam away.

When Steven was able to spear a fish, he would gobble down the eyes and organs. These parts provided moisture and important vitamins. Steven had to eat the fish raw, but food was food. Once, when a bird landed on his raft, Steven grabbed it and ate it raw, too.

On April 21, 1982, three fishermen saw some birds out over the water. Thinking the birds were feasting on fish, they headed their boat in that direction. As they got close, they thought they saw a tiny barrel bobbing in the water. It wasn't a barrel—it was Steven! After 76 days at sea, Steven was rescued.

Survival at Sea

May 26, 2010 — A huge wave hit my boat yesterday, swamping it with water. I barely had time to inflate my life raft before the boat sank. Now I'm nothing but a tiny speck in a vast expanse of water. I have few emergency supplies, but I do have a solar still. If I can keep it working, I can change salt water to fresh water and prevent dehydration.

June 15, 2010 — All emergency food supplies are gone, but I did spear a triggerfish that came to eat the barnacles that now cover the bottom of my raft. The flesh was bitter, but I swear it was the sweetest thing I've ever eaten! I ate the moist organs first to help prevent dehydration. I cut what I couldn't eat into strips and hung them out to dry.

June 21, 2010 — I'm so weak that yesterday I ripped a hole in my raft with my spear gun when I was wrestling with a fish. I've tried several patches, but nothing is working. I'm hip-deep in water.

June 26, 2010 — It took me five days to devise a successful patch made up of a bent fork, part of a shirt, and some rope. I have to add air to inflate the raft every 12 hours, but I can live with that!

July 5, 2010 — Rescued by a fishing boat! I said "Thanks" to the fishermen, but they said, "No, thanks!" to my dried triggerfish!

Directions: Fill in the bubble next to each correct answer.

1. **A person is in danger of becoming dehydrated if he or she**

   (A) does not have enough food.

   (B) does not have enough water.

   (C) does not have a solar still.

   (D) does not have emergency supplies.

2. **About how long was Steven adrift?**

   (A) one-and-a-half months

   (B) two-and-a-half months

   (C) three-and-a-half months

   (D) four-and-a-half months

3. **What do both stories have in common?**

   (A) They are both about sharks.

   (B) They are both about bitter fish.

   (C) They are both about being adrift.

   (D) They are both about moist organs.

4. **Describe the action Steven took when he saw the following**

shark	fish	bird

5. **Write in the date when the event occurred in "Survival at Sea."**

   a. made a patch with a fork _____

   b. rescued by fishing boat _____

   c. cut triggerfish into strips _____

   d. ripped hole in the raft _____

   e. huge wave hit boat _____

Counterfeit Chocolate

When you think of chocolate, you most likely think of things like cakes and cookies and candy bars. Most likely, you did not think of fake money! Strange as it may seem, there is a story that connects chocolate to counterfeit, or fake, money.

Long ago, the Mayans lived in Central America in what is present-day southern Mexico, Guatemala, and Belize. The Mayan people prospered between 250–925 A.D. During that time, the Mayans learned to brew some seeds that came from a tree native to their area. They brewed the seeds to make a very special drink. Today, we know this tree as the cacao tree. We use its beans, or seeds, to make all things that are chocolate.

Cacao beans were very valuable to the Mayans. They were traded for goods and used as an accepted form of payment. When scientists dug up old Mayan sites, they found counterfeit cacao beans! The beans had been made out of clay! They also found cacao bean husks. Counterfeiters had removed some of the beans from the husks. They had replaced the beans with sand!

The spread of chocolate began in the 16th century. This was when European explorers first carried the cacao beans back to Europe. Cacao beans are not used as money today, but we pay money for the chocolate made from them.

The Fake Masterpiece

For their field trip, Amanda's class traveled by train to an art museum. The director of the museum was showing Amanda's class around. He stopped in front of one painting surrounded by an ornate frame. The painting was of a woman sitting by a table with a rosy-cheeked baby on her lap. There was a bowl of apples and pears on the table, and a pineapple was beside the bowl.

The director said, "This painting is a European masterpiece from the country of Italy. It was painted in the 1300s. We only have the painting on loan. We are trying to raise funds so we can buy it. We want to buy it so we can add this magnificent old masterpiece to our permanent collection."

Amanda spoke up. She said, "You shouldn't buy it. The painting is counterfeit."

The director gasped. He said, "How could you say such a thing? You are only a child. You know nothing about the history of Italian art."

"It's true that I don't know anything about Italian art," said Amanda, "but still I know the picture is fake. Pineapples are native to Central and South America. They didn't come from Europe. A pineapple couldn't be in an authentic Italian painting from the 1300s because at that time no one in Europe had ever seen a pineapple!"

Directions: Fill in the bubble next to each correct answer.

1. **The beans from the cacao tree are**

   (A) clay.

   (B) seeds.

   (C) ancient.

   (D) counterfeit.

2. **Amanda knew**

   (A) the painter had to have seen a pineapple.

   (B) no fruit was brought to Italy until after the 1300s.

   (C) about the history of early Italian and European art.

   (D) paintings of pictures with pineapples were counterfeit.

3. **What do both stories have in common?**

   (A) counterfeit foods

   (B) foods found in masterpieces

   (C) what foods all explorers ate

   (D) foods native to Central America

4. **Think about when things happened in the story. Fill in the boxes to show what order they happened in the story.**

1.	2. *director shows the class around*	3.

6.	5.	4. *Amanda says painting is fake*

5. **Circle the region on the map to show where cacao came from. Draw an arrow to show where it spread to during the 16th century.**

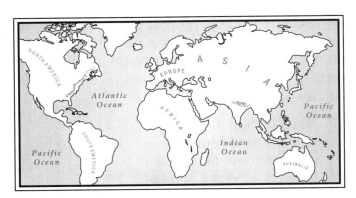

Nonfiction

Six Days of Survival

Scott O'Grady's F-16 jet had just been hit by an enemy missile. Surrounded by flames, Scott pulled on his ejector handle. He was ejected out of the burning plane into the air, five miles (8 km) above enemy ground.

The date was June 2, 1995. Scott was on a peacekeeping mission. He was keeping the airspace above Bosnia clear. Bosnia was a war zone. Now, an unknown enemy below had fired a missile that had destroyed his jet.

Scott fell through the air, his parachute open above him. Scott knew the enemy could see his parachute, and he knew they would be looking for him. Scott knew he would have to hide. He just hoped that his fellow soldiers could find him before the enemy did.

Scott carefully moved from hiding place to hiding place. He slept only in short spurts, keeping the time someone could creep up on him to a minimum. Cold, thirsty, and hungry, Scott gobbled down leaves and ants when he could find them. He gathered rainwater in a sponge for drinking.

Six days passed before Scott was located by his radio beacon. A rescue helicopter was sent to pick him up. The helicopter came under fierce enemy fire, but the soldiers on board fired back. They did not stop until Scott was on-board and safe.

Fiction

The Pilot's Survival Kit

Jenna raised her hand. She said, "Mr. Tolar, a fighter pilot wears a survival kit to use if for some reason he or she has to eject from the plane. I understand why the kit has packs of water. I understand why the kit has a heavy waterproof covering called a tarp. I understand why it has camouflage netting and a foil space blanket, and I understand why it has a knife. But why in the world does it have a plastic bag and a sponge? The pilot is trying to survive, not clean!"

Mr. Tolar said, "Pilots have to go through survival training. For example, they are taught that ants are edible. Some leaves can be eaten, too. To check if a leaf is edible, a pilot first places the leaf on the outside and then the inside of his or her lips, checking for burning or tingling. If the pilot feels nothing, he or she then chews and samples a single leaf. If there is still no reaction, the pilot can try eating more."

Mr. Tolar continued, "Pilots are also taught that it is important to stay hydrated. They must drink water, and the sponge and the plastic bag help prevent dehydration. When it rains, a pilot can wipe up water from leaves and other surfaces with the sponge. Then, he can squeeze the water into the bag, saving it for later."

Directions: Fill in the bubble next to each correct answer.

1. How was Scott located?

(A) by his F-16 jet

(B) by his parachute

(C) by his movements

(D) by his radio beacon

2. If a pilot places a leaf on the inside of his or her lip, it means that the leaf

(A) is edible.

(B) will be chewed and sampled.

(C) did not burn the outside of his or her lips.

(D) will next be placed on the outside of his or her lips.

3. Most likely, Scott drank rainwater because

(A) eating leaves and ants had made him dehydrated.

(B) he needed to sample drops on the outside of his lips.

(C) he did not find enough edible leaves and ants to eat.

(D) his survival kit did not have water packs for six days.

4. Which item(s) from their survival kits help pilots do the following things?

stay dry: _____

stay warm: _____

stay hydrated: _____

stay hidden: _____

5. Usually, people carry water in canteens or bottles. Why do you think a pilot's survival kit has a plastic bag instead of a canteen? What does one item have over the other?

_____

_____

_____

_____

Snake on the Loose

A zookeeper was working in the Reptile House, cleaning a cage that contained a spitting cobra that measured three-and-one-half feet long. There was a tiny drain at one end of the cage sealed by a rubber stopper. The zookeeper removed the drain's stopper so that water could go down the drain. Then, a radio call came in asking for assistance. The zookeeper went to help.

When the zookeeper returned to the cobra cage, the cobra was gone! In the zookeeper's rush to help, he had forgotten to put the drain plug back in! Somehow, the snake had squeezed its way into the drain! The zookeeper quickly made a sign and hung it on the door of the Reptile House. The sign said, "Closed for Repairs."

Zookeepers set baited hooks. They spread talcum powder out on every flat surface. They checked every day for signs that the snake had slithered past. Zookeepers checked out every snake "sighting." One sighting turned out to be a broken fan belt on a highway.

The cobra was found 40 days after it got loose. It was in a crawl space of the Reptile House. The funny thing about the escaped snake is what it did to zoo attendance. Knowing that a snake was loose, you might think that attendance would go down. Instead, the number of visitors to the zoo shot up!

A Clever Escape

"Orangutans eat fruit, right?" asked Ben as he walked into the kitchen.

"They sure do," answered his Aunt Opal. "In fact, they are the largest mammals in the world that survive mainly on fruit. They spend about eight hours a day looking for food."

Ben's aunt looked at him as he opened up a bag and began to fill it with oranges, apples, and bananas. "What are you doing to do," she joked, "feed an orangutan?"

"Well," said Ben, "I think there might be one sleeping on my bed. It must have climbed up the tree outside my window."

His aunt started to laugh. "Ben," she said, "you don't have to make up stories to get food. Here, if you're that hungry, take these peaches, too."

"Thanks," said Ben, rushing out of the kitchen.

When Ben's mother came home from work she said, "Where's Ben? I want to tell him about an unbelievable orangutan who keeps escaping. It took a while for the zookeepers to figure out how he was doing it. He was picking his lock with a bent wire that he hid in his mouth between escapes! Even more unbelievable is how the orangutan got the wire. He traded his biscuits for it to the orangutan in the next cage that was being put on a diet!" She continued, "He just escaped again last night!"

Directions: Fill in the bubble next to each correct answer.

1. **The cobra was found a little over**

   (A) one month after it got loose.   (C) three months after it got loose.

   (B) two months after it got loose.   (D) four months after it got loose.

2. **You cannot tell from the story that orangutans**

   (A) can climb trees.

   (B) eat mostly fruit.

   (C) spend about eight hours every day sleeping.

   (D) are bigger than other mammals that eat mostly fruit.

3. **One reason there were sightings of the snake outside the zoo might be that**

   (A) baited hooks had been put out.

   (B) news of the escape was on the nightly news.

   (C) the Reptile House was closed 40 days for repairs.

   (D) the powder showed signs of a snake slithering past.

4. **You are not told that the orangutan is in Benjamin's room, but as you read, you become sure that it is. Write down three things from the story that make you think there really is an orangutan in Benjamin's bed.**

   a. _____

   b. _____

   c. _____

5. **What would you do if you found a snake or an orangutan in your room? Would you go into your room? Would you try and feed the animal? Would you act the same for each animal? Tell why or why not.**

   _____

   _____

   _____

   _____

A Man and His Words

Abraham Lincoln was born on February 12, 1809, in a small log cabin in Kentucky. He grew up to become the 16th president of the United States. He was first elected in 1860, and then he was elected to a second term in 1864. Lincoln was shot and killed while serving his second term. He died on April 15, 1865.

Lincoln is famous for many things. He is famous for his honesty. He is famous for freeing the slaves. He is famous for his words. Some of his speeches are thought to be among the greatest in history. In one of his speeches, Lincoln said, "A house divided against itself cannot stand." Lincoln also spoke of "government of the people, by the people, for the people." It was Lincoln who spoke of "a new birth of freedom."

One comment of Lincoln's is not as well known as his speeches, but it shows Lincoln's wit. It shows his sense of humor. Lincoln was visited by hundreds of people every day. Some wanted jobs or money or help. Others just wanted to shake his hand.

In 1863, Lincoln came down with a mild case of smallpox. Smallpox is a disease. It is highly infectious. When something is infectious, it is easily spread. What did Lincoln say? He said, "Now I have something I can give to everyone."

What They Said

Mrs. Ramos said, "Class, when you quote something, you repeat exactly the words of another person or the words from a piece of writing. I'll say three quotations. Listen and tell me if you know who said them."

Mrs. Ramos said, "I've never been lost, but I was bewildered once for three days."

The students started to laugh. Natu said, "Bewildered means 'confused' or 'puzzled.' I wonder how many days somebody has to be bewildered before they are lost!"

Mrs. Ramos said, "The person I quoted would probably never think he was lost! It was Daniel Boone. Boone was born in 1734, and he blazed the Wilderness Road."

Mrs. Ramos said, "Now, my second quote was said by a man who was born in 1942. He said, 'Float like a butterfly, sting like a bee.'"

Linda said, "I know who you're quoting! The boxer Muhammad Ali said that. He also called himself 'The Greatest.' He was the heavyweight champion three times. Ali moved so fast that he seemed to float like a butterfly. His sharp punches stung like a bee."

"Very good," said Mrs. Ramos. "Now, start thinking, and get ready to sweat. After all, 'Genius is one percent inspiration and ninety-nine percent perspiration.'"

"Can we quote you on that?" asked Rachel.

"No," said Mrs. Ramos, "you can quote Thomas Edison, the inventor born in 1847. He said it."

Directions: Fill in the bubble next to each correct answer.

1. **Lincoln came down with smallpox**

   Ⓐ before he was elected president.

   Ⓑ after he was reelected president.

   Ⓒ while he was serving his first term.

   Ⓓ while he was serving his second term.

2. **Who said, "Float like a butterfly, sting like a bee"?**

   Ⓐ a boxer   Ⓒ an inventor

   Ⓑ a president   Ⓓ a trail blazer

3. **Which quote comes closest to meaning "Strength comes in staying together"?**

   Ⓐ "Now I have something I can give to everyone."

   Ⓑ "A house divided against itself cannot stand."

   Ⓒ "I've never been lost, but I was bewildered once for three days."

   Ⓓ "Genius is one percent inspiration and ninety-nine percent perspiration."

4. **Name three things for which Abraham Lincoln is famous.**

   a. _____

   b. _____

   c. _____

5. **Choose one of the quotations in either of the two stories. Tell who said it, what it means, and why you like it.**

   _____

   _____

   _____

   _____

The Weary Hounds

After discovering a fox raiding his chicken coop in broad daylight, a farmer gave chase with his six hounds. In hot pursuit, the hounds quickly trailed the fox up a hill. At first the farmer ran alongside of his hounds, but at the top of the hill the farmer realized he was too weary to continue.

Remaining at the top of the hill, with a full view of what was going on below, the farmer watched the fox run into a hollow log and out the other end. The farmer watched as his hounds picked up the fox's scent at the end of the log the fox had exited from and continue the chase. The farmer saw the fox lead the hounds in a large circle before returning to the log.

The farmer saw the fox enter and exit the log at different ends, each time leading the dogs in wide circles before returning. The farmer was amazed at the fox's endurance. The fox seemed fresh, but the dogs were exhausted. They were weary from the constant running. How could it be that the fox had so much more endurance than the hounds?

Then, the farmer figured out. Running down the hill, he ran to the hollow log and poked inside of it with a stick. A fox jumped out! All along, there had been two foxes! While one fox took a turn leading the hounds in circles, the second fox had rested!

Aesop's Crow

Aesop was a Greek storyteller who lived long ago. He wrote fables, short stories with morals, or lessons. Aesop's fables often involved animal characters who could talk. "The Fox and the Crow" is an example of such a fable. It goes like this:

A crow was sitting high on a branch of a tree with a large, delectable, sweet smelling piece of cheese in her beak. A fox came by, and as he passed beneath the tree, he looked up and saw the enormous piece of cheese in the crow's mouth.

With his mouth watering at the thought of swallowing the delectable tidbit, the fox said, "Oh, what a beautiful bird I see above me! There can be no other avian creature of her equal. Her plumage is gorgeous, her feathers glossy and iridescent in the sun. If only her voice is as sweet as her looks are fair, then surely she must be Queen of the Birds!"

Hugely flattered, the crow wanted to show the fox that she could indeed sing as sweetly as her looks were fair. She opened her mouth and gave a loud "Caw!" As soon as the crow opened her mouth, the cheese dropped out, and the fox gobbled it up. After the cheese was eaten, the fox informed the crow that although she could sing, she had no wits.

What is Aesop's moral for this fable? The moral is, "Beware of flatterers."

Directions: Fill in the bubble next to each correct answer.

1. **What do both stories have in common?**

   (A) They both are about smart characters.

   (B) They both are about fresh flatterers.

   (C) They both are about morals or lessons.

   (D) They both are about animals with endurance.

2. **Something that has endurance**

   (A) is weary.

   (B) has a scent.

   (C) can last a long time.

   (D) can be figured out.

3. **The fox said that the crow had no wits because she**

   (A) didn't figure out why he was flattering her.

   (B) didn't think she could be Queen of the Birds.

   (C) didn't know that no other bird could be her equal.

   (D) didn't sing in a voice as sweet as her looks were fair.

4. **Tell what each fox was doing.**

   Fox 1: _____ leading the hounds in a big circle _____

   Fox 2: _____

   Fox 1: _____

   Fox 2: _____ leading the hounds in a big circle _____

5. **Think about the beginning, middle, and end of the fable in "Aesop's Crow." Very briefly, write in some of the story details.**

Beginning	Middle	End

Nonfiction

The Power of Gold

Ejnar Mikkelsen was a Danish explorer. In 1907, he was coming back from the far North after exploring parts of Alaska that were unknown to Europeans. Now, on his return trip, he was on a sled heading south to Nome, Alaska. To his surprise, he saw three men coming toward him. The men were walking, hunched over in the cold. They were only wearing clothes fit for a warm house.

Ejnar could see that the men were already frostbitten. He told the men to turn back, warning them that continuing on would only invite death. Ejnar offered the men a ride on his sled, but the men angrily refused! They had heard of a gold strike and were struck by gold fever. They wanted to be among the first to the Klondike gold fields they were sure were just up ahead. Ejnar was not strong enough to force the men to return.

A few hours later, Ejnar came to a hut filled with gold-seekers. Ejnar asked for volunteers to go back with him and look for the three men. Ejnar said that if enough of them went, they could hopefully save the men's lives by forcing them to return.

Ejnar and the volunteers struggled through the blizzard, but they were too late. They found the three men frozen solid, close to where Ejnar had first come upon them.

Fiction

Winter in a Gold Town

These days I am making more money in Dawson washing clothes and doing other people's laundry than I ever could at home. Here, the stores have scales so that people can pay in gold dust or money. Most people pay in gold dust. Sometimes, at the end of the day, I can scoop up over 20 dollars of gold dust from the bottom of my washtub!

It seems everything but the gold has to be imported. Vegetables and fruits have to be shipped in from far away. It's very expensive to import things.

Things are better now that they were a month ago, when we were at the end of the long, hard winter of 1899. Waiting for the ice to melt and for boats to come down the Yukon River was tough. We were starved for everything, even news! One newcomer auctioned off a newspaper from Seattle that was over one month old. A clever miner bought the newspaper for 50 dollars. Then, he charged people one dollar each to listen as it was read out loud! Over 100 people paid to listen!

You have never seen such determined gold miners. They cross steep mountain passes while carrying heavy packs. They have to carry their own wood if they want to light a fire. Too many don't think about what they really need. They only think about gold when they should be thinking about how to survive.

Directions: Fill in the bubble next to each correct answer.

1. **Why did Ejnar tell the men he met that continuing on was to invite death?**

   (A) The men were not dressed for a blizzard.

   (B) Ejnar wanted to get to the gold fields first.

   (C) The men were heading to unknown parts of Alaska.

   (D) Ejnar did now know how many volunteers would help him.

2. **When something is imported, it is**

   (A) very expensive.   (C) a fruit or vegetable.

   (B) used by volunteers.   (D) brought in from far away.

3. **What do both stories have in common?**

   (A) determined gold miners   (C) explorers of the far North

   (B) men who did not feel cold   (D) scales used to weigh gold dust

4. **List in order what Ejnar does in the story. Use the numbers 1 to 5. Put "1" by what happened first. Put "5" by what happened last.**

   _____ heads south to Nome, Alaska

   _____ asks for volunteers to bring the men back

   _____ tells men they are inviting death

   _____ finds three men frozen to death

   _____ meets three men on their way to the Klondike gold fields

5. **Think about what it would be like to live in the gold town of the second story. Would you rather be a miner looking for gold or a person who made money by supplying services to the miners? Explain your answer.**

   _____

   _____

   _____

   _____

   _____

The Underground Town

In 1915, 14-year-old Willie Hutchison disobeyed orders and left camp. Willie was in South Australia on an expedition led by his father. The expedition was in desperate need of water. It was a matter of life or death. Willie had been told to remain in camp while the other expedition members went searching for a source of the vital liquid.

All the men returned to camp. No one had found water. They were very worried about Willie, especially when he failed to return by dark. Finally, Willie strolled in carrying a sugar bag over his shoulder. The sugar bag was half-full, but it wasn't full of sugar. It was full of precious gems! Willie had found opals! He had also found some water.

A mining town sprang up where Willie discovered the opals. It is called Coober Pedy. The name comes from the Arabana Aboriginal language. It comes from the words "kupa piti." Loosely, these words mean "white man in a hole." Most of Australia's opals are mined here.

Today, there are about 3,500 people living in Coober Pedy. Most of them live under the ground. Hotels and churches are under the ground. Museums, stores, and restaurants are all under the ground, too. This is because Coober Pedy is blazing hot during the day. Temperatures have often hit 122°F (50°C) and above! At night, it is freezing cold. Under the ground, people can live at a constant comfortable temperature.

The Lucky Kick

I live in Coober Pedy, and I was playing golf with my friends at the only golf course in town. The golf course and its fairways are all black, with not even one blade of grass to cover them. That's because the course is made of oiled sand. I was about to hit the ball when my brother rode up and said, "Mum says it's your turn to wash the dishes."

I was angry, but I knew I had to go home and wash the dishes. Mum always told us we should feel like royalty when we washed dishes because water was so expensive and hard to get. I didn't care if water cost as much as liquid gold. I certainly didn't feel like a king when I was scrubbing away at leftover food!

I followed my brother down under the ground. It was a relief to get out of the blazing heat of the sun, but the pile of dirty dishes was very upsetting. I was so angry that I kicked the doorjamb with my boot. I let out a cry of horror as the rock began to crumble. Then I yelled, "Mum, Dad, come quick!"

Everyone came running and looked in wonder at the opal showing beneath the crumbling rock. Scraping away in excitement, Dad said, "I've never seen such a big opal! This single stone will sell for at least 20 thousand dollars!"

Directions: Fill in the bubble next to each correct answer.

1. **From the stories, you can tell that**

   (A) water is more expensive than oil.

   (B) royal dishes are washed in liquid gold.

   (C) some opals are buried underneath the ground.

   (D) finding an opal is easier than finding water.

2. **Why did the boy in "The Lucky Kick" kick the doorjamb?**

   (A) He was angry that he was not royalty.

   (B) He was angry that the dishes were dirty.

   (C) He was angry that water was so expensive.

   (D) He was angry that he had to wash the dishes.

3. **Most likely, the golf course in Coober Pedy was made of oiled sand because**

   (A) the temperature was not constant.   (C) there was not enough water for grass.

   (B) opals were mined at the golf course.   (D) grass would not grow under the ground.

4. **Fill in the boxes about the town's name.**

Name of Town	Comes From (name of language)	Sounds Like (words in that language)	Meaning of Name (in English)

5. **Think about when things happened in the story. Fill in the boxes to show what order they happened in the story.**

1.	2. *brother rides up*	3.

6.	5.	4. *kicks doorjamb*

Answer Key

Practice 1 Questions (page 5)
1. D
2. D
3. B
4. A
5. Answers will vary. Accept reasonable responses.

Practice 2 Questions (page 7)
1. A
2. C
3. B
4. feline: cat; canine: dog; reptile: snake; rodent: mouse, rat, capybara.
5. The large front teeth should be circled. Accept reasonable responses.

Practice 3 Questions (page 9)
1. B
2. C
3. C
4. sap – c; size of overalls – d; pockets – b; receipt – a
5. A

Practice 4 Questions (page 11)
1. C
2. D
3. D
4. The paw with the nails out and the face with the tear lines should be circled.
5. Answers will vary. Accept reasonable responses.

Practice 5 Questions (page 13)
1. B
2. C
3. A
4. C
5. Answers will vary. Accept reasonable responses.

Practice 6 Questions (page 15)
1. B
2. C
3. D
4. Accept appropriate responses.
5. A

Practice 7 Questions (page 17)
1. D
2. D
3. C
4. 3, 5, 2, 1, 4
5. body – A; tail – B; top of head – F

Practice 8 Questions (page 19)
1. C
2. C
3. B
4. B
5. Answers will vary. Accept reasonable responses.

Practice 9 Questions (page 21)
1. A
2. C
3. B
4. different: male/female, skin color; same: unlike others in Corps, helped Lewis and Clark

5. Answers include swam to a sandbar to gather greens and searched Clark's blanket for fleas every day.

Practice 10 Questions (page 23)
1. B
2. A
3. C
4. Frog 1: no, rainforests of Central and South America, tree leaves; Frog 2: yes, Japan, dull lab light
5. A

Practice 11 Questions (page 25)
1. A
2. B
3. C
4. B
5. swimming: 2.4 miles (4 km); bicycling: 112 miles (180 km); running: 26 miles, 385 yards (42.2 km)

Practice 12 Questions (page 27)
1. B
2. B
3. A
4. submarine – iron fish; dive bomber – sparrow hawk; America – our mother
5. Answers will vary. Accept reasonable responses.

Practice 13 Questions (page 29)
1. A
2. D
3. B
4. C
5. Answers will vary. Accept reasonable responses.

Practice 14 Questions (page 31)
1. C
2. D
3. D
4. Answers will vary. Accept reasonable responses.
5. Answers will vary. Accept reasonable responses.

Practice 15 Questions (page 33)
1. B
2. A
3. C
4. shark: annoyed it by stabbing it with spear gun; fish: gobbled down its eyes and organs when he speared it; bird: grabbed it when it landed and ate it raw
5. a. June 26, 2010; b. July 5, 2010; c. June 15, 2010; d. June 21, 2010; e. May 26, 2010

Practice 16 Questions (page 35)
1. B
2. A
3. D
4. 1. field trip to art museum; 3. director tells class about painting; 5. director tells Amanda she knows nothing about Italian art; 6. Amanda says Italian artists would not know about pineapple in the 1300s

5. Check map for answers. Central America (the area between North America and South America) should be circled. An arrow should be drawn from Central America to Europe.

Practice 17 Questions (page 37)
1. D
2. C
3. D
4. dry: tarp; warm: foil space blanket; hydrated: water packs, sponge, plastic bag; hidden: camouflage netting
5. Answers will vary. Accept reasonable responses.

Practice 18 Questions (page 39)
1. A
2. C
3. B
4. a. Ben gets fruit.; b. Ben tells his aunt that he think there is one on his bed.; c. Ben's mom hears that one has escaped from the zoo.
5. Answers will vary. Accept reasonable responses.

Practice 19 Questions (page 41)
1. C
2. A
3. B
4. Answers could include his honesty, freeing the slaves, his speeches/words, being president, etc.
5. Answers will vary. Accept reasonable responses.

Practice 20 Questions (page 43)
1. A
2. C
3. A
4. Answer on both lines should be, "resting in a hollow log."
5. Beginning: fox wants cheese in crow's mouth; Middle: fox flatters crow; Ending: crow sings and cheese falls down to fox

Practice 21 Questions (page 45)
1. A
2. D
3. A
4. 1, 4, 3, 5, 2
5. Answers will vary. Accept reasonable responses.

Practice 22 Questions (page 47)
1. C
2. D
3. C
4. Coober Pedy; Arabana Aboriginal language; kupa piti; "white man in a hole"
5. 1. playing golf; 3. follows brother under the ground; 5. rock crumbles; 6. finds expensive opal

Grade 5

Wonders

CALIFORNIA Content Reader

B

The McGraw·Hill Companies

 Macmillan/McGraw-Hill

Published by Macmillan/McGraw-Hill, of McGraw-Hill Education, a division of The McGraw-Hill Companies, Inc.,
Two Penn Plaza, New York, New York 10121.

Printed in the United States of America

3 4 5 6 7 8 9 10 073 12 11 10 09

Contents

Contents

Chemical Reactions

Matter is made of elements, which are made of atoms. An **element** is a substance that cannot be further simplified. Elements are the simple substances that combine to make all other substances. Some common elements are carbon, aluminum, oxygen, and iron.

Elements are made of tiny invisible particles called atoms. An **atom** is the smallest particle that has the properties of an element. We might obtain one if we could only cut a small piece of aluminum foil in half about 50 times.

We would then have a speck of aluminum less than a billionth of an inch in size. Each element is made of one kind of atom. This means all the atoms in an element have the same structure. Some elements are heavy, others are light. Some elements are shiny, and some are opaque. A few elements are magnetic, but most are not. These and many other properties of elements are determined by the structure of their atoms.

Matter is constantly changing around you. Water vapor forms clouds, tree leaves fall and rot, and foods in the kitchen are cooked. A starting substance in a chemical reaction is called a **reactant** (ree•AK•tuhnt). The new substance is called a **product.** We say that reactants yield products, and we write it as

reactants ⟶ **products**

Composition of Aluminum

aluminum foil

When matter undergoes a physical change, no new substances are formed. When matter undergoes a chemical change, a chemical reaction occurs. In a **chemical reaction**, substances change into new substance.

Chemical reactions may occur between atoms, molecules, or compounds. A common example of a chemical equation is the one showing the formation of carbon dioxide (CO_2). The diagram below shows a chemical reaction between carbon (C) atoms and oxygen (O_2) molecules. The reactants, carbon and oxygen, are chemically changing into a product, carbon dioxide. Fire provides the energy needed for molecules to be rearranged.

The total mass of the reactants always equals the total mass of the products. Since the mass of the substances is the mass of their atoms, the total number of atoms remained the same. For instance, the same number of atoms are in the reactants and the products shown below.

Atoms simply rearrange into new combinations. The change in combinations of atoms is what gives products new and different properties. Atoms are neither gained nor lost during chemical changes. They are always conserved.

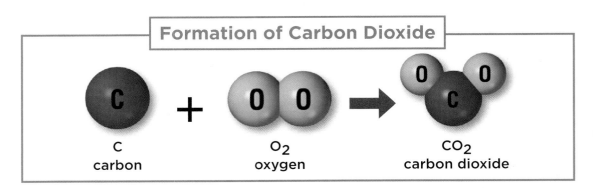

Formation of Carbon Dioxide

C
carbon

O_2
oxygen

CO_2
carbon dioxide

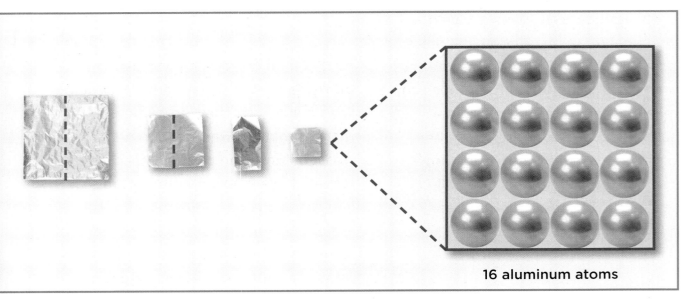

16 aluminum atoms

Mr. Mix-It

For one man, mixing chemistry and clay leads to new discoveries—toys!

Todd Bigelow/
Aurora

▲ **Chemist Maelo Cordova shows off one of his slimiest inventions.**

Sometimes Maelo Cordova spends the day shaping modeling clay. Other times he tries out doll makeup or races miniature cars. Surprisingly, Cordova is not a kid. He's a chemist. He uses his knowledge of chemistry to make toys.

As a kid in Puerto Rico, Cordova asked questions. What is in shampoo that helps it clean hair? How can I mix cleaning products to get out spots? In high school, Cordova discovered the name of his hobby: chemistry. He loved learning how substances combine to make new stuff.

The process he loves is called a chemical reaction. A chemical reaction occurs when two or more substances are mixed together. In the process of mixing, the atoms in the original substances break apart. They then combine to make a new substance. The starting substances are called reactants. The results of the reaction are called products.

Cordova studied chemistry in college. He now works for a big toy company.

At work, Cordova mixes chemicals and performs experiments. But he does his homework first. "I like to spend time investigating what I'm looking for before I get in the lab," Cordova explains.

For one project, he was asked to make icky, sticky play slime. His recipe was a little off. The goo came out harder than he wanted, and he almost tossed it into the trash. Instead he saved it. He later patented his mistake. He called the new invention flubber. Says Cordova, "In science, you never throw anything away." His next mistake may turn out to be even more fun.

It's Elemental

Everything in the world is made of different combinations of elements. An element is a substance that contains only one kind of atom. It can't be broken down into a simpler substance. A compound is a combination of two or more elements. Some compounds are familiar. One of these is sodium chloride. It is a combination of the elements sodium and chlorine. You know it as table salt.

Charles D. Winters/Photo Researchers, Inc.

▲ Chemistry is all about combining elements.

Light Up the Night

Some chemical reactions produce light. One example is a toy you may have seen. It is a plastic tube that glows in the dark. The tube is filled with a liquid substance. When you bend the tube, a small container inside it breaks. This releases another substance. A chemical reaction between the two substances takes place. The product of the reaction is light. The light makes the dye in the tube glow in the dark.

Photolibrary.com pty. Ltd./Index Stock

Great Chemistry

This table lists some famous chemists and their achievements.

Name	Birth Date	Country of Birth	Achievement
Robert Boyle	1627	England	First to use scientific methods to study chemistry
Irene Curie	1897	France	Created new radioactive elements
John Dalton	1766	England	Discovered theory of matter based on atoms
Antoine Lavoisier	1743	France	Discovered oxygen and that water is made of oxygen and hydrogen
Dimitri Mendeleyev	1834	Russia	Arranged all known elements in a chart called the periodic table
Alfred Nobel	1833	Sweden	Invented dynamite, an explosive

Description Writing Frame

Use the Writing Frame below to orally summarize "Chemical Reactions."

Elements are the simple substances that combine to make all other substances.

For example, some common elements are _____

_____.

Elements are made of tiny invisible particles called _____.

During chemical reactions, the atoms in the reactants _____

_____

_____.

For example, fire causes a chemical reaction between carbon (C)

atoms and oxygen (O_2) molecules. The reactants, _____

_____ are changed into the product _____

_____.

Use the frame to write the summary on another sheet of paper. Be sure to include **bold** signal words. Keep this as a model of this Text Structure.

Critical Thinking

1 A starting substance in a chemical reaction is called a
_____ .

    A. reaction

    B. product

    C. reactant

2 Point to the sentence in "Mr. Mix-It" that tells what sodium chloride is.

3 Find the paragraph in "Chemical Reactions" that explains elements. Point to one common element.

> A table presents a large amount of information, such as names and numbers, in a compact way.

4 What does the table on page 9 tell you about chemists? Discuss this table with a partner.

Digital Learning

For a list of links and activities that relate to this Science standard, visit the California Treasures Web site at www.macmillanmh.com to access the Content Reader resources.

Have children view the Science in Motion Video "Formation of Carbon Dioxide."

EL In addition, distribute copies of the Translated Concept Summaries in Spanish, Chinese, Hmong, Khmer, and Vietnamese.

The Periodic Table

The **periodic table** arranges all the known elements in a chart of rows and columns of increasing atomic number. Note how the different colors are used to show the three different groups of elements. These groups are the metals, the metalloids, and the nonmetals.

The columns in the periodic table are called groups, or families. The rows are called periods. Families of elements have similar properties. For example, the halogens are found in one column. The noble gases are found in another one. Elements change from metals to nonmetals as you go from left to right across the periodic table. They also develop more metallic properties as you go down any family.

You may have noticed there are two rows separated from the periodic table. These rows include the rare earth elements. Many of these elements are synthetic, or man-made.

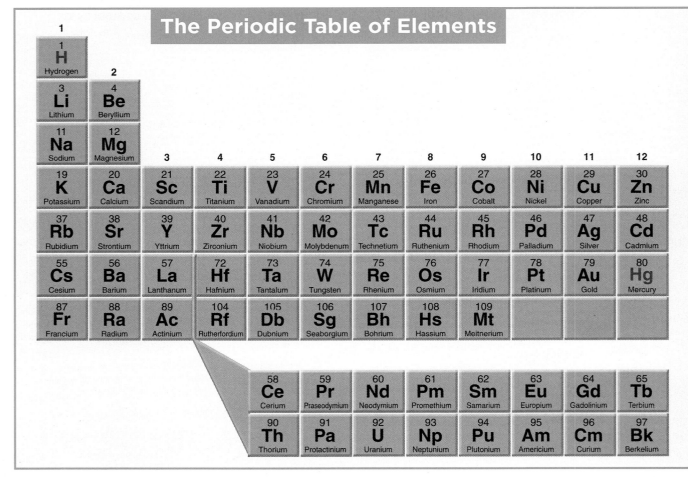

The Periodic Table of Elements

About three fourths, or 75%, of the elements on the periodic table are metals. The metals fill the left and center of the periodic table. Among those you might be familiar with are metals such as gold (Au), copper (Cu), silver (Ag), zinc (Zn), aluminum (Al), iron (Fe), lead (Pb), mercury (Hg), magnesium (Mg), and chromium (Cr). A **metal** is an element that is a good conductor of heat and electricity. When metals are polished, they reflect most of the light that strikes them. This gives metals a shiny appearance or luster.

The melting points of metals are spread over a wide range of temperatures. This makes them useful for many purposes. Mercury, for example, has a melting point of –39°C (–38.2°F) and is a liquid at room temperature 25°C (77°F). A column of liquid mercury about 760 mm (30 in.) high is used in barometers. The air pressure is measured by the height of the mercury column in millimeters.

Metals with high melting points are useful because they can withstand high temperatures. Aircraft and spacecraft, for example, often have metal parts that are made of titanium (Ti). This element can take the heat—titanium melts at 1,668°C (3,034°F)! It is also lightweight and strong, an added plus for a flying craft.

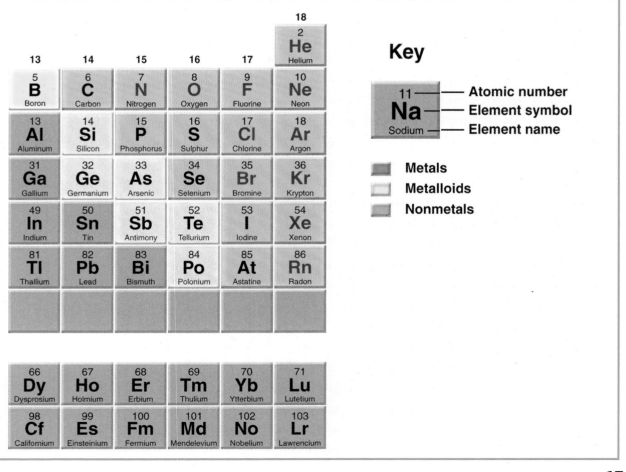

Richard Serra: *Artist*

▲ Richard Serra and one of his works of art

Some people use steel to erect buildings or make machines. Others use steel to make art.

Richard Serra used to fling ladles full of hot lead at the wall. He won awards for doing it. Serra is an artist. Lead is just one of the materials he uses to express his ideas.

As a young man, Serra made his sculptures out of fiberglass and rubber. But he worked in a steel mill to make money to help pay for college. At the steel mill, he got to know a lot about metal. When he graduated, he started to work with lead, iron, and steel.

When Serra started throwing molten lead against the wall in the name of art, people took notice. Later, he decided that it would be interesting to work with huge metal objects and gravity. He created gigantic lead plates and pipes called "prop pieces." They got their name from the fact that he propped them up against one another without using anything else to hold them up. One of the best known of these pieces was called "One Ton Prop (House of Cards)." The piece was just four squares of lead leaning against one another to form a cube. With nothing else holding it up, the cube really was like a delicately balanced house of cards. It didn't fall, but if it had, it would have made a tremendous crash!

As Serra became more famous, he was paid to create sculptures for outdoor parks. He used big steel plates to build a series of sculptures called "Torqued Ellipse." These sculptures are made up of steel plates, 13 feet high, formed into twisted ovals with a gap on one side to allow viewers to enter.

The twisted ovals were so popular that Serra was asked to create even more outdoor sculptures. He created huge steel spirals and rippling bands of steel. He built spaces in which visitors could wander, exploring the texture and shape of space.

Though Serra does nothing to the surface of the steel, he bends it at high temperatures and leaves it out in the rain. As a result, the surfaces of his pieces are covered with stress patterns; splatter stains; and long, shallow ruts. Then, they rust. They look a little like a weathered cliff and a little like a painting.

Richard Serra was asked to put on a one-man show at New York City's Museum of Modern Art. First, though, museum staff had to make sure the floors wouldn't fall in. After all, just one of Serra's pieces weighs 243 tons. (An average airplane weighs just 199 tons!) —*Lisa Jo Rudy*

▼ **Serra creates his sculptures by bending steel at very high temperatures.**

Jose Simal/epa/Corbis

A museum visitor explores Serra's work from the inside.

Thos Robinson/Getty Images

Sequence Writing Frame

Use the Writing Frame below to orally summarize "Richard Serra: Artist."

Richard Serra is a famous artist. When he was young he **first** made

his sculptures out of _____

_____ .

Then _____

_____ to help pay for college.

After college, Serra started working with _____

_____ .

Later, Serra decided to work with _____

_____ .

Then Serra was paid to _____

_____ .

Today Richard Serra is famous.

Use the frame to write the summary on another sheet of paper.
Be sure to include the **bold** signal words. Keep this as a model of
this Text Structure.

Critical Thinking

1　An element that is a good conductor of heat and electricity is
_____ .

    A. magnet

    B. metal

    C. magnesium

2　Find the paragraph in "The Periodic Table" that explains the melting points of metal.

3　Point to the sentence in "Richard Serra: Artist" that tells what happens when Serra leaves his steel out in the rain.

4　Discuss the periodic table on page 12 with a partner. What do the different colors mean?

A table presents a large amount of information, such as names and numbers, in a compact way.

Digital Learning

For a list of links and activities that relate to this Science standard, visit the California Treasures Web site at www.macmillanmh.com to access the Content Reader resources.

Have children view the e-Review "Metals and Alloys."

EL In addition, distribute copies of the Translated Concept Summaries in Spanish, Chinese, Hmong, Khmer, and Vietnamese.

Mixtures and Microscopes

A **mixture** (MIKS•chuhr) is a physical combination of two or more substances that do not form new substances.

Since a mixture contains at least two different substances, no mixture is pure. The properties of a mixture blend the properties of its parts. For example, muddy water—a mixture of clay and water—gets you both dirty and wet. Powdery clay alone can get you dirty, water alone can get you wet, and the mixture can do both.

We classify mixtures according to certain properties. In heterogeneous mixtures, separate particles are big enough to see. Trail mix and tossed salad are examples of heterogeneous mixtures.

Mixtures that look the same throughout are homogenous mixtures. In homogeneous mixtures, the particles are too small to see. Milk, a liquid, and cream cheese, a solid, are examples of homogeneous mixtures. They both look the same throughout because you can't see the individual particles.

Some mixtures separate by themselves when their parts settle into layers. We call this type of mixture a **suspension** (suh•SPEN•shuhn).

A suspension is a mixture whose particles settle and separate within a few hours. In some suspensions, particles settle into layers quickly. Oil and vinegar as a salad dressing, for example, can be shaken into a smooth-looking mixture. However, the oil forms a layer on top of the vinegar in a matter of minutes.

If the particles in a mixture are the size of atoms or molecules, the mixture is called a **solution** (suh•LEW•shuhn). This happens when one substance dissolves in another, like sugar in water. All solutions are homogeneous, which means they have the same makeup throughout. Solutions may be colored, but if they are liquid or gas, they are always transparent, like window cleaner solution or air.

When mixed together, oil and vinegar are an example of a suspension.

The field ion microscope was invented in 1951. Atoms appear as bright spots.

It is hard to believe just how small the particles in some mixtures are. Suppose you put a pinch of salt in your hand. In that little bit of salt there are more than a billion atoms, half of which are sodium atoms and half chlorine atoms. So atoms are much too small for us to see with just our eyes.

However, microscopes have allowed scientists to "see" atoms. An **electron microscope** uses electron beams instead of light to produce images. The electrons are aimed at a sample. When an electron hits an atom and bounces back, an image is formed. The first electron microscope was invented in 1932. It was the first time scientists could see large molecules.

The **field ion microscope** was invented in 1951. This microscope works similarly to the electron microscope, but instead of electrons it uses ions, which are particles with an electric charge. The field ion microscope

is even more powerful than the electron microscope, and it helped scientists to see atoms for the first time.

Modern versions of the microscope have given scientists an atom-by-atom view of metals. This technology shows that atoms have a spherical shape. Atoms look like fuzzy balls through a field ion microscope. The images don't actually show the protons, neutrons, and electrons that you see in atom diagrams. Looking at the behavior of these particles helps scientists determine their shapes and positions inside the atom.

The field ion microscope only shows large atoms and molecules. However, this problem was partially overcome by the invention of the scanning tunneling microscope. The scanning tunneling microscope uses a very fine metallic tip to examine samples.

Name That Powder

A laser light invention helps keep Americans safe.

Ever since the destruction of the World Trade Center in 2001, the United States has been on high alert for terrorism. The Department of Homeland Security is on the lookout for anything that could be used to harm American citizens.

In 2001, envelopes stuffed with powdered anthrax (a deadly spore) were mailed to several members of Congress and TV anchors. A number of postal workers got sick, and several died. So far, the anthrax case has not been solved.

That's why Homeland Security gets involved when unidentified powders and mixtures turn up. The powder could be harmless but it could also be a bioweapon. Diseases such as anthrax and salmonella can be placed in the food or water supply.

Up until now, the only way for Homeland Security to figure out what they had found was to send a sample to a laboratory. Days or weeks later, they'd get an answer. So far, no bioweapons have been used on the American people. But what if a bioweapon did cross the border, or show up in our food supply? How could Homeland Security figure it out fast enough?

Workers wear protective clothing while investigating a potential biohazard outside a U.S. post office.

www.usps.com

The answer to this riddle is a device called the Raman spectrometer. Raman spectrometers bounce laser light off of the molecules that make up an object or substance. Most of the light bounces back unchanged. Some of the light, though, changes color. The Raman spectrometer analyzes the changes in light. Then it compares what it finds to a library of "light signatures" programmed into its system. Finally, the spectrometer identifies the object or substance.

One company has taken Raman spectroscopy to a new level. A machine that used to sit in a lab can now be carried around and powered with batteries. The new machine costs about $30,000. Its inventor, Daryoosh Vakhshoori, says you can use it to "read the substance as if it had a bar code, observing if the white powder you see is sugar, aspirin, or something more dangerous."

Raman spectrometers can also analyze substances found deep beneath the sea or inside the human body. They can monitor the level of oxygen in blood, analyze what looks like a skin cancer, or identify a virus.

The portable version was used after Hurricane Katrina, in New Orleans, Louisiana. Cleanup crews used it to figure out what was in the sludge left on streets after floodwaters drained away. Now, a new system called SORS (spatially offset Raman spectroscopy) can read molecules through plastic packaging and other soft materials. Raman spectrometers may be at work at an airport, in a laboratory, or on city streets near you right now. —Lisa Jo Rudy

▲ **Daryoosh Vakhshoori and his portable spectrometer**

Sludge left by Hurricane Katrina could have contained hazardous material. ▶

Compare/Contrast Writing Frame

Use the Writing Frame below to orally summarize "Mixtures and Microscopes."

A mixture is _____ .

All mixtures are the **same** because no _____ .

However, there are ways that mixtures are different. They are **different**

because in heterogeneous mixtures, the particles _____

_____

_____ .

In homogeneous mixtures, the particles _____ .

_____ .

There is another way mixtures are **different**. In a _____ ,
the particles settle and separate within a few hours. In **contrast**, in a

solution _____ .

So, mixtures have similarities and differences.

• • • • • • • • • • • • • • • • •

Use the frame to write the summary on another sheet of paper.
Be sure to include **bold** signal words. Keep this as a model of this
Text Structure.

Critical Thinking

1. An electron microscope uses _____ to produce images.

   A. light

   B. heat

   C. electron beams

2. Find the word from "Mixtures and Microscopes" that describes how scientist "see" atoms.

3. Point to the place in the text "Name That Powder" where it talks about how bioweapons could be used.

4. Refer to the photo on page 20 and discuss with a partner how the caption helps you understand the text.

> Photographs and captions help you understand content in an informational article.

Digital Learning

For a list of links and activities that relate to this Science standard, visit the California Treasures Web site at www.macmillanmh.com to access the Content Reader resources.

EL Have children view the e-Review "Mixtures."

In addition, distribute copies of the Translated Concept Summaries in Spanish, Chinese, Hmong, Khmer, and Vietnamese.

The States of Matter

Look at all the matter around you. Books, tables, houses, and trees are made of matter. Milk, oil, and raindrops are made of matter. Tires, balloons, basketballs, and your room are matter.

What makes these examples of matter different? One difference between these examples is the state of matter. A **state of matter** is one of the three forms that matter can take: solid, liquid, or gas.

Books, tables, houses, and trees are examples of solids. Milk, oil, and raindrops are examples of liquids. Tires, balloons, basketballs, and your room contain gas. All matter is made of particles. The behavior of the particles of matter determines its state.

The particles of a solid usually line up in an organized pattern. They vibrate back and forth but do not move past one another. They "wiggle" in relatively fixed positions. Because the particles in a solid are not moving around, their shape and volume do not change.

The diagram of the solid shows how the particles are packed together tightly.

You can not compress a solid. This is because it has no room between its particles.

The particles of a liquid move more than they do in the solid state. They have more freedom of motion and can move past one another. However, they still remain relatively close together.

The diagram of the liquid illustrates the behavior of the basic particles in a liquid. Since the particles of a liquid can flow, the shape of liquid takes on the shape of its container. If there is no container, the liquid spreads out as far as it can. The volume of a liquid remains the same because the particles do not separate from one another.

Gases consist of particles that move very rapidly. The particles are widely spread out and have lots of empty space between them. They are able to take up such a large volume because of their motion. They move faster when hot and slower when cool.

In the gas diagram, the particles move around freely so their volume and shape fit the shape and volume of the container. If there is no container, gases keep spreading further and further apart.

solid

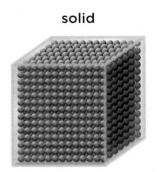

liquid

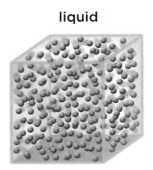

gas

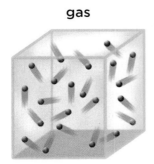

Common Elements

All living things share common elements. Plants have thick cell walls and many woody structures to provide support. Cell walls and woody tissue are made mainly of carbon, hydrogen, and oxygen, which explains why these three elements are so common in plants.

Like plants, animals are composed mainly of carbon, hydrogen, and oxygen. The amounts of elements typical for animals are shown in the chart.

Animal bodies contain a great deal of water. In fact, about 60% of human body weight is water. A lot of our oxygen and hydrogen comes from the water in our bodies. Other than bones and teeth, the rest of our tissues are mainly made of carbon, oxygen, hydrogen, nitrogen, phosphorus, and a dash of chlorine and sulfur. So really, carbon, hydrogen, and oxygen are the three main elements shared by all living things.

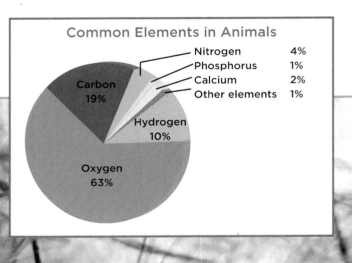

Common Elements in Animals

Element	Percent
Nitrogen	4%
Phosphorus	1%
Calcium	2%
Other elements	1%
Carbon	19%
Hydrogen	10%
Oxygen	63%

▼ Plants and animals are made mainly of carbon, hydrogen, and oxygen.

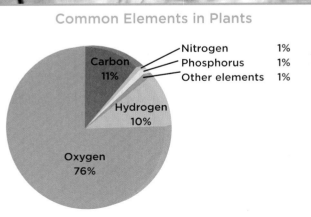

Common Elements in Plants

Element	Percent
Nitrogen	1%
Phosphorus	1%
Other elements	1%
Carbon	11%
Hydrogen	10%
Oxygen	76%

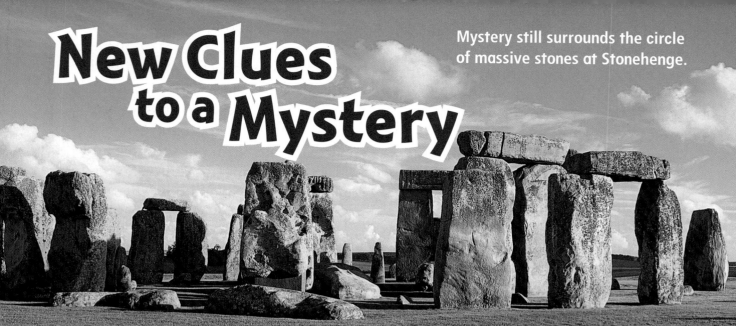

New Clues to a Mystery

Mystery still surrounds the circle of massive stones at Stonehenge.

Scientists are trying to solve an ancient mystery that has puzzled people for hundreds of years.

Peter Adams/Getty Images

The Stonehenge World Heritage site is located in southern England. Stonehenge is a circle of large, standing stones. We know that the stones are arranged to line up with the Sun during the summer and winter solstices. But Stonehenge remains a puzzle. No one knows exactly how it was built. The huge stones each weigh several tons. The people who built Stonehenge had to move them long distances. Archaeologists have now put a major piece of the puzzle in place.

Prehistoric Homes

The puzzle piece is a prehistoric village. It is located about two miles from Stonehenge. Scientists think they found the houses where the people who built Stonehenge lived. They dug up the floors of eight wooden houses. Arrowheads, stone tools, and human and animal bones were also found. There may be hundreds more houses in the area.

The scientists tested material from the village to find out how old it is. They used a test called carbon dating. The test showed that the village is about the same age as Stonehenge. Both are about 4,500 years old.

Adam Stanford/Aerial-Cam

Scientists have found the remains of an ancient village near Stonehenge. ▶

Radioactive Carbon (C14) and Carbon Dating

Radioactive carbon (C14) is absorbed from the air by plants. When animals eat the plants, C14 enters their bodies. Humans take in C14 by eating animals and plants. We have the same percentage of C14 atoms in us as all living plants and animals have.

When a plant, animal, or human dies, it stops taking in C14. The C14 that is in it starts to decay. It decays slowly and steadily. Scientists can figure out how old something is by measuring how much C14 is left in it. They know that C14 has a half-life of 5,730 years. This means that it takes 5,730 years for half of the C14 to decay. After about 50,000 years the amount of C14 remaining will be so small that the object's age can't be determined.

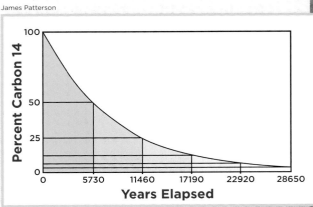

James Patterson

▲ **The amount of C14 in something that once lived reveals how long ago it died.**

Connecting the Dots

The ancient village is located in an area known as Durrington Walls. Archaeologists can now see how Stonehenge and Durrington Walls may have been connected. Both sites have stone avenues that lead to the Avon River (see map). The river could have been used for travel from one location to the other. Researchers think that the ancient villagers visited Stonehenge for religious observances.

"We knew these [sites] were from broadly the same period," says Julian Thomas, the project's director. What scientists didn't know was that the sites were so closely connected. "[That] completely changes our understanding of Stonehenge."

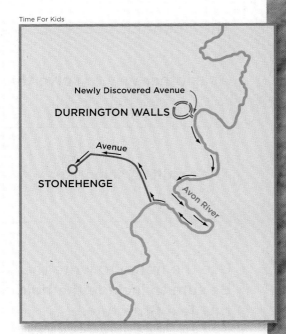

Time For Kids

▲ **This map shows how people might have used the Avon River to travel between the ancient village and Stonehenge.**

Problem/Solution Writing Frame

**Use the Writing Frame below to orally summarize
"New Clues to a Mystery."**

Scientists are trying to solve the mystery of Stonehenge.

The **problem** is no one knows how _____

_____

because the people had to move _____

_____.

To help solve this problem, a scientific team dug up _____

_____.

They found _____.

As another way to **solve this** problem, scientists used _____

_____ to see how old the village was.

The **result** is, scientists _____

_____.

Use the frame to write the summary on another sheet of paper.
Be sure to include the **bold** signal words. Keep this as a model of
this Text Structure.

Critical Thinking

1 Which is not a form that matter can take?

    A. Air

    B. Liquid

    C. Solid

2 Find the sentence in "New Clues to a Mystery" that explains how humans take in radioactive carbon.

3 Point out the paragraph in "The State of Matter" that describes the behavior of the basic particles in a liquid.

4 How does the map on page 27 support the text of "New Clues to a Mystery?"

Maps are drawings of geographic locations such as a city, state, or park.

Digital Learning

For a list of links and activities that relate to this Science standard, visit the California Treasures Web site at www.macmillanmh.com to access the Content Reader resources.

Have children view the e-Review "Properties of Matter."

EL In addition, distribute copies of the Translated Concept Summaries in Spanish, Chinese, Hmong, Khmer, and Vietnamese.

Plant and Animal Cells

Plants, animals, and all living things are made of cells. A **cell** (SEL) is the smallest unit of a living thing that can carry out the basic processes of life. Grass and mountain lions are made of cells. Your own body is made up of trillions of these tiny building blocks.

▼ This mountain lion and the grass are made of many cells.

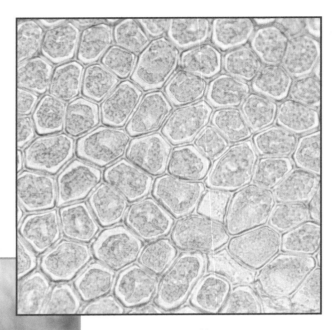

▲ plant cell

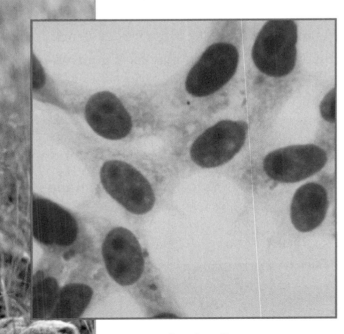

▲ animal cell

The cells of different living things are similar in many ways. All cells need energy to carry out life processes. All cells have structures, called **organelles** (awr•guh•NELZ) that work together to help them perform life processes. These organelles have jobs that must be done to keep the cell alive.

The cells of living things also have some important differences. For example, many plants need to grow tall to reach the sunlight. This means they need something in their cells to provide extra support. Plants can't move around to find water when it doesn't rain. So plant cells need to be able to store a lot of water. Plants usually don't eat other living things, so their cells need special organelles to produce their own food.

Unlike plants, animals move around from place to place. They need cells that are more flexible and allow more movement. Since animals can move to find water, their cells do not need to store as much water as plant cells. Animals do not have cells that produce their food. They must get their energy from eating other living things.

A DINO BONE BREAKTHROUGH

What do a T. rex dinosaur and a chicken have in common? Scientists may have the answer.

In 2003 scientists in Montana dug up a *Tyrannosaurus rex* (T. rex) fossil. Many dinosaur remains have been found in the same area. This T. rex fossil was 70 million years old. When alive, it was 40 feet tall and probably weighed five tons. Its thighbone was huge.

A Very Lucky Break

To fit the thighbone onto a helicopter, paleontologists had to break it in half. They took the T. rex thighbone into their lab at North Carolina State University. First they soaked the fossil in weak acid. The acid removes minerals that have formed over millions of years. The surprise came when scientists saw what was left in the part of the bone that once held the marrow. It was a clear stretchy material. "It was totally shocking," said team leader Mary Schweitzer. Such material had never before been found in a dinosaur bone. Usually any soft parts of a dead animal disappear completely. But that hadn't happened in this T. rex's thighbone.

Under an electron microscope, scientists examined the stretchy material. They saw tiny blood vessels and reddish-brown dots. They believe these dots are the nuclei, or central structures, of blood cells.

"Bone is living tissue, . . . and has to have a very good blood supply," said Schweitzer. The scientists also saw what looked like bone-building cells. Bone tissue in our bodies is constantly being rebuilt by bone cells. Here was evidence that the same process may have gone on in T. rex's bones.

Tissue from the T. rex thighbone returns to its original shape after being stretched.

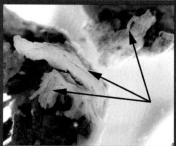

Areas of the bone have bundled strands of tissue which had never before been seen in such an old fossil.

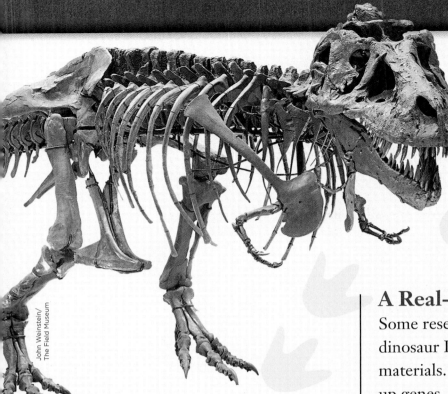

John Weinstein/
The Field Museum

A Real-Life Jurassic Park?

Some researchers hope to recover dinosaur DNA from the T. rex thighbone materials. DNA is the chemical that makes up genes. That makes some dinosaur fans curious. Could the DNA be used to clone dinosaurs? Could a real Jurassic Park ever exist?

Hans-Dieter Sues, a paleontologist, says no. "But," he adds, "there's lots of biological information locked in this material."

Dr. Schweitzer and her team of paleontologists are looking beyond their Montana T. rex. They are investigating other dinosaur sites around the world. They hope to find more dinosaur fossils containing tissue samples. —*Joe McGowan*

T. Rex's Descendants

The T. rex thighbone is providing new clues about dinosaurs. Scientists reported that its blood vessels are almost identical to those in modern ostrich bones. This could support the theory that today's birds are descended from dinosaurs.

Another team of scientists has studied material from the T. rex thighbone. They recently published a report on their work. They think T. rex is related to another modern bird—the chicken! "Based on the small sample we've recovered, chickens may be the closest relatives [to T. rex]," says John Asara, co-leader of the team. Frogs and newts are also listed as modern relatives of T. rex.

Chickens may be T. rex's closest living relatives. ▶

Compare/Contrast Writing Frame

Use the Writing Frame below to orally summarize "Plant and Animal Cells."

The cells of plants and animals are **alike** in many ways. They are

alike because all cells need _____.

They are also **alike** because they both have structures called

_____.

In some ways, however, _____ and

_____ are **different**. They are **different**

because plant cells _____

_____.

They are also **different** because animals need cells _____

_____.

So _____ and _____
cells are **alike** in some ways and **different** in others.

Use the frame to write the summary on another sheet of paper.
Be sure to include **bold** signal words. Keep this as a model of this
Text Structure.

Critical Thinking

1 The smallest unit of a living thing that can carry out the basic processes of life is a _____.

   A. organelle

   B. cell

   C. atom

2 Point to the sentence in "A Dino Bone Breakthrough" that explains what the reddish brown dots might be.

3 Find the paragraph in "Plant and Animal Cells" that tells why animals need cells that are flexible.

4 Study the photograph on page 32. Discuss with a partner why the tissue samples are important.

> Photographs and captions help you understand content in an informational article.

Digital Learning

For a list of links and activities that relate to this Science standard, visit the California Treasures Web site at www.macmillanmh.com to access the Content Reader resources.

Have children view the Science in Motion Video "Cells to Organisms."

EL In addition, distribute copies of the Translated Concept Summaries in Spanish, Chinese, Hmong, Khmer, and Vietnamese.

The Respiratory and Circulatory Systems

Your **respiratory system** is made of a series of tubes and passages that transports the air you breathe. It allows an exchange of gases between the air, your blood, and your tissues.

When you **inhale** (in•HAYL), or breathe in, air enters your body through your mouth and nose. Your **lungs** are organs that fill with air when you inhale. They expand like balloons. Then they empty of air when you **exhale** (eks•HAYL), or breathe out. This movement is controlled by the contractions of a large, flat sheet of muscle called the **diaphragm** (DIGH•uh•fram). Air is drawn down into your lungs through a series of narrowing branched tubes. The tubes are surrounded by **capillaries** (KA•puh•ler•eez). A capillary is a tiny blood vessel. Oxygen from the air in the tubes enters the blood cells in the capillaries. They take the oxygen to the rest of your cells.

As blood passes through the lungs, it takes in oxygen and releases carbon dioxide. As you know, carbon dioxide is a waste product of cellular respiration. Along with water vapor, carbon dioxide is exhaled out of the body through the respiratory system.

The **circulatory system** is the transport system made up of the heart, blood vessels, and blood. This system is also known as the cardiovascular (kahr•dee•oh•VAS•kyuh•luhr) system.

Your circulatory system is like a postal system for your body, with the blood cells bringing things to and from your body cells. Your heart is a muscular organ that is constantly pumping blood through your body.

First, blood from your heart is pumped into your arteries (AHR•tir•eez). An artery carries blood mixed with oxygen away from your heart. Your organs, tissues, and cells take the oxygen, food, and nutrients they need from your blood. They also release waste into your blood. Oxygen and waste, like carbon dioxide, move in and out of your blood through the walls of your capillaries. From the capillaries, the blood carrying carbon dioxide moves into your veins (VAYNS). A vein takes the blood cells carrying carbon dioxide back to your heart.

Circulation and Respiration

Your circulatory and respiratory systems work together to transport oxygen and carbon dioxide through your body.

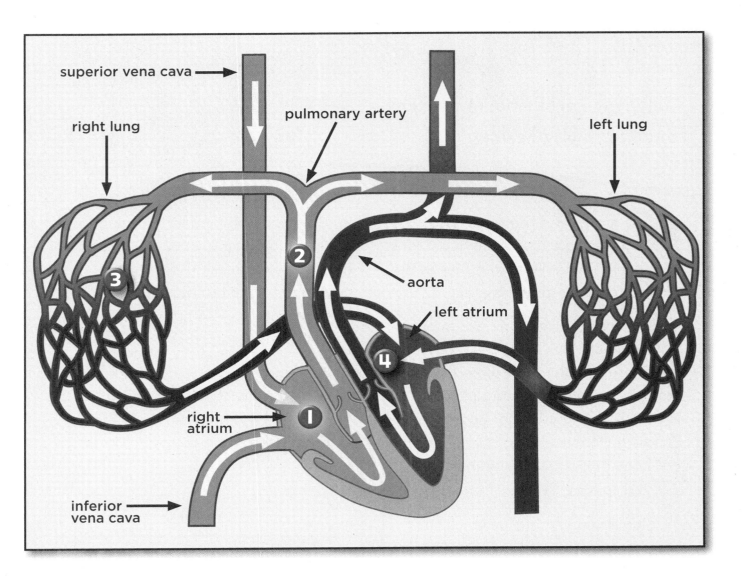

1. Carbon dioxide-rich blood from the superior vena cava and inferior vena cava enters the right atrium. Then it flows into the right ventricle and is pumped out through the pulmonary artery.

2. The carbon dioxide-rich blood flows through the pulmonary artery into the lungs.

3. In the lungs, the blood drops off carbon dioxide and picks up oxygen.

4. Oxygen-rich blood from the lungs flows into the left atrium through the pulmonary veins. Then it goes into the left ventricle where it is pumped out to the body through the aorta.

How to Stay Fit for Life

Getting the right amount of exercise is key to staying healthy.

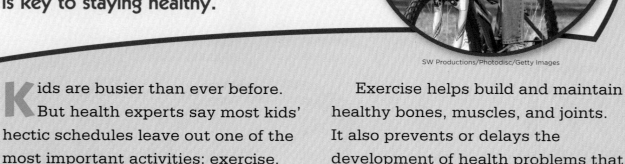

SW Productions/Photodisc/Getty Images

Kids are busier than ever before. But health experts say most kids' hectic schedules leave out one of the most important activities: exercise.

"It's a myth that kids get enough physical activity," gym teacher Andy Schmidt says. Schmidt was once named Teacher of the Year by the National Association for Sport and Physical Fitness. "Kids' lives are busy, but they don't get the exercise time needed to stay healthy."

This trend is a big factor in the rising rate of obesity among kids. School budget cuts and more emphasis on preparing for tests have led many schools to cut down on gym and recess time.

Exercise helps build and maintain healthy bones, muscles, and joints. It also prevents or delays the development of health problems that affect adults, including high blood pressure and heart disease.

The good news: Riding bikes and rollerblading with friends count too. "Have fun, and do what you enjoy," Schmidt says. —*Ritu Upadhyay*

Many kids today don't get enough exercise. ▶

Corbis

38

A Formula for Staying Fit

Different parts of the human body require different types of exercise. Here are combinations for staying strong and flexible.

Todd Bigelow/Aurora/Getty Images

AEROBIC EXERCISE
Running, basketball, jumping rope, dancing

BENEFIT
Strengthens your heart and lungs and improves the delivery of oxygen and blood throughout your body.

AMOUNT
Thirty minutes a day, five days a week

STRENGTH TRAINING
Pull-ups, sit-ups, push-ups, tug-of-war

BENEFIT
Building muscle strength and endurance improves overall fitness.

AMOUNT
Two or three days a week

FLEXIBILITY TRAINING
Sit and reach, yoga, gymnastics, Tai Chi

BENEFIT
Flexibility allows you to move joints and stretch muscles in a full range of motion.

AMOUNT
Before and after any workout

Michelle Pedone/zefa/Corbis

MM Productions/Corbis

Julie Toy/Getty Images

More than half of girls and one-quarter of boys ages 6 to 17 cannot run a mile any faster than they can walk one.

Cause/Effect Writing Frame

**Use the Writing Frame below to orally summarize
"How to Stay Fit for Life."**

There are **several reasons** many young people are not exercising
on a regular basis.

One reason is because _____.

Another reason is schools have _____

_____.

This explains why _____
is rising among kids.

Exercising helps build and maintain _____

_____.

It also prevents or delays the development of _____

_____ and _____.

More _____
and self-confidence are also a **result** of exercise.

For all of these reasons, it is important that kids _____

_____.

Use the frame to write the summary on another sheet of paper.
Be sure to include the **bold** signal words. Keep this as a model of
this Text Structure.

Critical Thinking

1. A tiny blood vessel is a _____ .

    A. vein

    B. artery

    C. capillary

2. Point to the sentence in "How to Stay Fit for Life" that tells the benefit of strength training.

3. Find the paragraph in "The Respiratory and Circulatory Systems" that explains what happens when you inhale and exhale.

4. What does the diagram on page 37 of "The Respiratory and Circulatory Systems" tell you about your body? Discuss with a partner.

Diagrams help readers see, or visualize, difficult information in a text.

Digital Learning

For a list of links and activities that relate to this Science standard, visit the California Treasures Web site at www.macmillanmh.com to access the Content Readers resources.

Have children view the Science in Motion "Circulation and Respiration."

EL In addition, distribute copies of the Translated Concept Summaries in Spanish, Chinese, Hmong, Khmer, and Vietnamese.

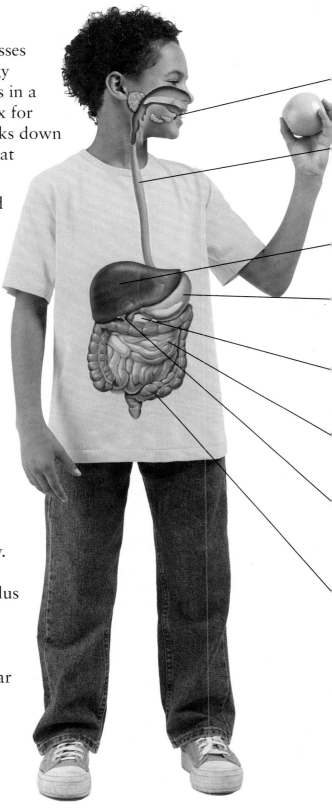

The Digestive System

Your cells need energy to perform life processes and do work for your body. They get this energy from the food you eat. Eating is like putting gas in a car. But the food you eat is too big and complex for your tiny cells. **Digestion** (die•JES•chuhn) breaks down the food into smaller and simpler substances that your body can absorb.

Your body breaks down food physically and chemically. When you take a bite of food, your teeth and tongue break down food physically by chewing it into smaller pieces. The salivary glands in your mouth and throat produce a watery fluid called **saliva** (suh•LIE•vuh). Saliva helps to moisten and soften the chewed food, or bolus (BOH•luhs), and break it down chemically.

Next, your tongue helps move the bolus to the **pharynx** (FAR•ingks), the name for the portion of the throat that connects the mouth to the digestive tube. Now you swallow, and the bolus passes into a long, muscular tube called the **esophagus** (i•SOF•uh•guhs).

The esophagus is lined with **mucus**, (MYOO•kuhs) which makes the inside slippery. The walls contain muscles that contract and expand like rubber bands. They squeeze the bolus along toward the **stomach** (STUH•muhk). It takes about ten seconds for a ball of food to move from the mouth to the stomach. The stomach is a digestive organ with thick muscular walls. Three layers of muscles in the stomach squeeze the food with wavelike motions.

Mouth The mouth is where digestion begins.

Esophagus The esophagus is a tube that connects your mouth to your stomach.

Liver The liver adds digestive juices to food.

Stomach The stomach is a hollow bag with muscular walls.

Pancreas The pancreas is an organ about 6 inches long that produces several digestive juices.

Small Intestine The small intestine connects the stomach and the large intestine. It absorbs digested food.

Gall Bladder The gall bladder is a pear-shaped organ that stores digestive juices produced by the liver.

Large Intestine The large intestine eliminates undigested waste.

The muscles of the stomach contract and relax to create the movement. While the stomach is moving, it adds mucus and digestive acids to the food. The muscles squeeze and mix the bolus until it is changed into a thick soupy liquid. After about four to six hours of mixing and squeezing, the liquid food is released into the small intestine (in•TES•tuhn).

The **small intestine** is a coiled, tubular organ that is connected to the stomach. Digestive juices continue to break down the nutrients from the food into smaller, simpler forms. The nutrients are then absorbed by the small intestine. To reach the blood, the nutrients pass through the walls of the small intestine and into tiny blood vessels. Blood carries the nutrients to the rest of the body by way of the circulatory system. The remaining undigested material moves on to the large intestine.

The **large intestine** is a thick, tubular organ that removes undigested waste. It is shorter and thicker than the small intestine. The **cecum** (SEE•kuhm) connects the large intestine to the small intestine. The **colon** (KOH•luhn) is the widest part of the large intestine. Some water and some minerals are absorbed in the colon and are carried to your body tissue by the blood.

The last part of the large intestine is the **rectum** (REK•tuhm) Solid waste called **feces** (FEE•seez) is stored in the rectum until strong muscles push it out of the body through the **anus** (AY•nuhs). This process is called **elimination** (i•li•muh•NAY•shuhn).

A LESSON IN CARING

A teacher's gift saves a student's life.

Jane Smith, a science teacher at a middle school in North Carolina, taught her students a lesson in generosity they won't forget.

A Student in Pain

When the school year began, Smith noticed that 15-year-old Michael Carter was wearing his pants really low. She suggested that he hike them up. Michael explained that wearing his pants low was more comfortable. His kidneys were hurting. Michael was born with a medical problem that kept his kidneys from working properly. By the time he met Smith, he was using a machine to help his kidneys. Several times a week it filtered impurities out of his blood.

"I Have Two. Do You Want One?"

Michael told Smith that he needed a kidney transplant. For a transplant to work, the tissues of the donor and the person receiving the kidney have to match. In Michael's case, no one in his family was able to be a donor.

Smith said, "I have two [kidneys]. Do you want one?" It turned out that Smith's tissue type matched Michael's. The transplant surgery was arranged. Both teacher and student recovered from the operations.

"Ms. Smith was our guardian angel," said Michael's mom.

Smith hoped her gift might inspire others to donate their organs.

Courtesy UNC Health Care

Jane Smith visits Michael Carter after the surgery.

What Do Kidneys Do?

The main function of our two kidneys is to filter out waste material from the blood. Kidneys also balance the levels of fluid and minerals in the body. They keep calcium levels constant and regulate blood pressure. Kidneys also play a role in creating red blood cells. For people who are otherwise healthy, one kidney can do the job of two.

What Happens When Kidneys Fail?

When kidneys fail, unhealthy waste materials build up in the body. This waste can cause illness and death.

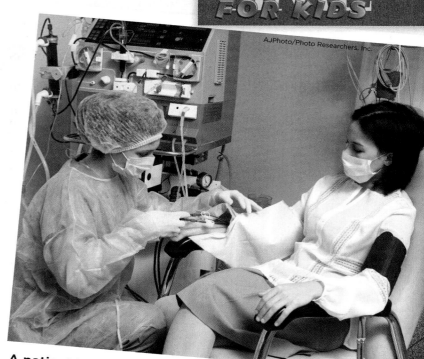

AJPhoto/Photo Researchers, Inc.

A patient is prepared for kidney dialysis.

People with kidney failure must have their blood filtered by a machine. The process is called dialysis. Kidney failure can't be cured. But damaged kidneys can be replaced with a healthy kidney. The donor and recipient can usually go on to lead healthy lives with one kidney apiece. *—Susan Moger*

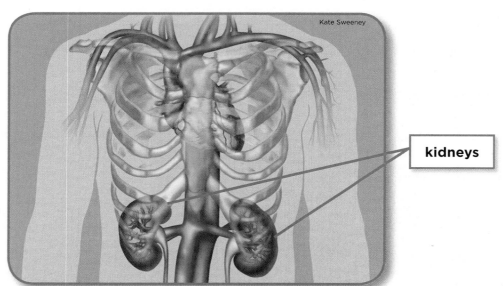

Kate Sweeney

kidneys

Sequence Writing Frame

Use the Writing Frame below to orally summarize "The Digestive System."

Digestion breaks down food into smaller and simpler substances that your body can absorb. When you take a bite of food, your teeth and tongue

_____ .

Next your tongue helps move the bolus _____

_____ .

Then you _____ and the bolus passes into the

_____ .

Next the bolus passes into the _____ .

About four to six hours **later**, _____

_____ .

Blood carries the nutrients from the small intestine to the rest of the body.

Then _____ .

Finally the _____
removes solid waste from the body.

Use the frame to write the summary on another sheet of paper.
Be sure to include the **bold** signal words. Keep this as a model of
this Text Structure.

Critical Thinking

1 The tube that connects the mouth and the stomach is

the _____ .

   A. pharynx

   B. esophagus

   C. intestine

2 Find the word from "The Digestive System" that describes the system that removes waste products from your body.

3 Point to the place in "A Lesson In Caring" that explains dialysis.

4 Refer to the diagram on page 45 and discuss the location of your kidneys.

Read the labels to find out what the diagram is about.

Digital Learning

For a list of links and activities that relate to this Science standard, visit the California Treasures Web site at www.macmillanmh.com/ to access the Content Readers resources.

Have children view the e-Review "The Digestive System."

EL In addition, distribute copies of the Translated Concept Summaries in Spanish, Chinese, Hmong, Khmer, and Vietnamese.

Photosynthesis and the Respiration Cycle

All living things need energy to carry out their life processes. The photosynthesis and respiration cycle provides energy to plants and animals.

Leaves capture and use energy from the Sun, water absorbed by the roots, and carbon dioxide from air to make food for the plant. This food making process is called photosynthesis (foh•tuh•SIN•thuh•sis).

The sugar that plants produce during photosynthesis is a **carbohydrate** (kahr•boh•HIGH•drayt). Carbohydrate is the name given to a group of substances made from carbon, hydrogen, and oxygen. Simple carbohydrates can be stored as food or modified to make structural materials.

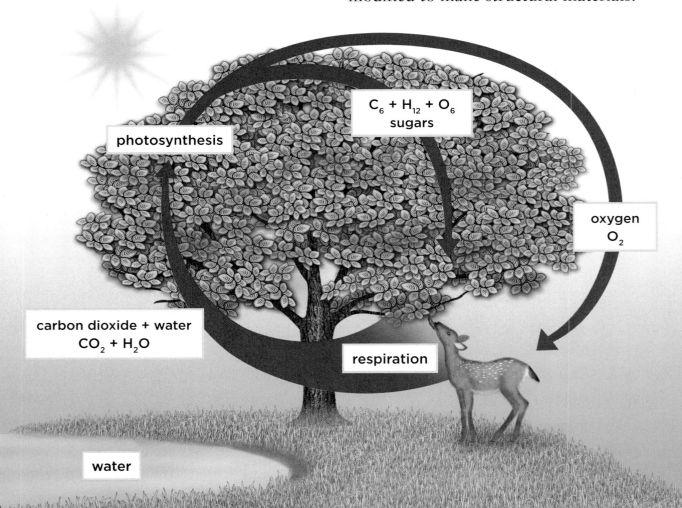

photosynthesis

$C_6 + H_{12} + O_6$
sugars

oxygen
O_2

carbon dioxide + water
$CO_2 + H_2O$

respiration

water

When plants store sugar, they usually store it as starch. The cell walls of plant cells are made of cellulose. Starch and cellulose are complex carbohydrates made of thousands of simple sugar units.

Animals also depend on photosynthesis as a source of energy. When an animal eats part of a plant, it takes in the carbohydrates stored in the plant. Even when animals are carnivores and eat other animals, they take in the carbohydrates that the other animals gained from eating a plant in the first place.

The oxygen that plants produce during photosynthesis is breathed in by animals during respiration. Some of the oxygen is also used by plants. When plant or animal cells need energy, they use oxygen to break down stored carbohydrates. This is a process known as **cellular respiration** (SEL•yuh• luhr•res•puh•RAY•shuhn).

You can think of respiration and photosynthesis as the opposite of each other. During cellular respiration, plant and animals cells produce carbon dioxide and water, which are then released back into the air. Plants use the water to produce sugars during photosynthesis. And the cycle begins again.

Cellular respiration occurs in mitochondria. Mitochondria provide the energy that plant and animal cells need to grow and to repair themselves. This is why they are known as the power house of the cell.

A typical cell holds about 1,000 mitochondria. Oxygen and sugar produced during photosynthesis enter the cell and go into the mitochondria. The mitochondria use oxygen to break down the stored carbohydrates to release energy. Carbon dioxide and water are also released as products of this reaction.

In the mitochondria, the released energy is changed into a substance called ATP. The ATP is like a battery that goes where the cell needs energy. These batteries are constantly being used. The energy that it takes for you to read this page is coming from ATP.

Are We Killing the Oceans?

Dead zones spread in the world's oceans.

The world's oceans are teeming with life, from microscopic organisms to whales, the largest animals on Earth. In a strange twist, human activity on land is creating "dead zones" in coastal waters around the globe.

Over the past four decades, dead zones have appeared in almost 150 places, mostly in Europe and the East Coast of the United States. Some are small and some are vast. The dead zone in the Gulf of Mexico is 8,000 square miles, or about the size of New Jersey.

No animals live in these areas because the water below the surface has no oxygen in it. Without oxygen, fish and other animals cannot survive.

Too Much of a Good Thing

The causes of ocean dead zones can be traced to places far from the coastline. Chemical fertilizer used on farms and lawns is the main cause. Pollution from power plants and other industries adds to the problem.

First, runoff caused by rain and soil erosion carries fertilizer and other chemicals into a river. Then the river carries them along to the ocean, and all the chemicals are dumped in one place. That's why ocean dead zones usually appear at the mouths of rivers. Giant river systems, like the Mississippi, collect runoff fertilizer from millions of square miles.

When fertilizer reaches the oceans, it feeds tiny plants called algae. The abundance of food causes massive algae blooms. The surface of the ocean can be covered with algae for hundreds of miles. When the algae die, they sink to the bottom and are eaten by bacteria.

Astromuff/Getty Images

This photo taken by a NASA satellite shows the Mississippi River carrying tons of sediment into the Gulf of Mexico.

Fertilizers and other chemicals can cause fish die-offs like this one.

The bacteria use oxygen and release carbon dioxide. As more and more algae die, more and more bacteria grow. Eventually the bacteria use up all the oxygen in the lower levels of the dead zone. Once all the oxygen is gone, nothing can live there. Like a broken scale, the ecosystem tips too far in one direction. There is no life at the bottom of the dead zones because there is too much life at the top.

Algae blooms like this are a major reason ocean dead zones form.

Saving the Oceans

Governments around the world have been trying to halt the spread of these oxygen-free areas. For example, in Europe, governments along the Rhine River have agreed to cut nitrogen levels in half. One solution is to plant trees and grasslands alongside rivers. The plants will soak up the fertilizer before it reaches the ocean. Reducing pollution from industry and untreated sewage would also make rivers cleaner. Finally, cutting the use of chemical fertilizer on farmlands and lawns would go a very long way toward solving the problem.

Problem/Solution Writing Frame

**Use the Writing Frame below to orally summarize
"Are We Killing the Oceans?"**

Human activity on land is creating dead zones in coastal
waters around the globe.

This problem occurs because runoff carries _____

_____.

When fertilizer reaches the oceans, it feeds tiny plants called

algae. **This is a problem because** _____

_____.

One solution is to _____.

The result is _____

_____.

Another solution is to reduce _____

_____.

This will **result** in cleaner rivers.

Use the frame to write the summary on another sheet of paper.
Be sure to include the **bold** signal words. Keep this as a model of
this Text Structure.

Critical Thinking

1 A carbohydrate is made from _____.

    A. sugar, oxygen, and water

    B. carbon, hydrogen, and oxygen

    C. carbon, helium, and oxygen

2 Find the sentence in "Photosynthesis and the Respiration Cycle" that explains the process that plants and animals use to break down stored carbohydrates.

3 Point to the place in the text of "Photosynthesis and the Respiration Cycle" where it shows you how respiration helps photosynthesis.

4 Refer to one of the photographs on page 51. Orally create a new caption explaining the photograph.

> Photographs and captions give visual examples that help explain what the text states.

Digital Learning

For a list of links and activities that relate to this Science standard, visit the California Treasures Web site at www.macmillanmh.com to access the Content Readers resources.

Have children view the Science in Motion "Photosynthesis and Respiration."

EL In addition, distribute copies of the Translated Concept Summaries in Spanish, Chinese, Hmong, Khmer, and Vietnamese.

Changing States of Water

Oceans cover most of Earth's surface. An **ocean** is a large body of salt water. The oceans cover about 70% of Earth's surface. The remaining 30% of the surface is mostly land. Other bodies of water cover a small fraction of the surface.

Water on Earth can exist in three different forms, or states. When you drink a glass of water, you are using water in the liquid state. When you put ice cubes in your glass, you are using water in the frozen state. The water you breathe out with each breath is in the gaseous state.

Where can you see water changing states? Look at what happens to the water in a pond as a year goes by. As fall turns to winter, the cooling temperature removes heat from liquid water, causing it to freeze into solid water. As winter turns to spring, the warming temperature adds heat to the frozen water, causing the ice to melt.

Changes in State of Water in a Pond

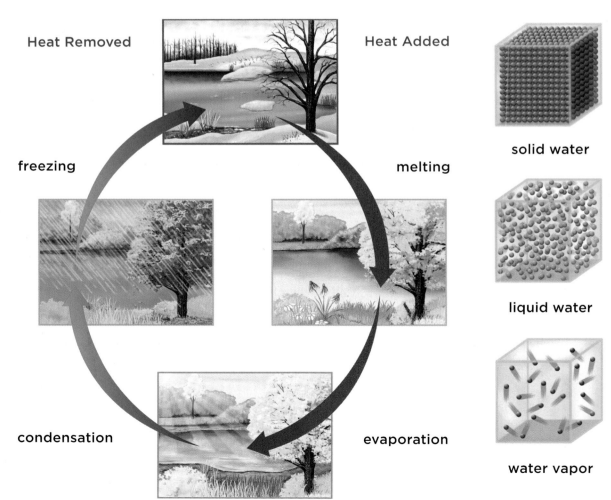

Heat Removed

Heat Added

freezing

melting

condensation

evaporation

solid water

liquid water

water vapor

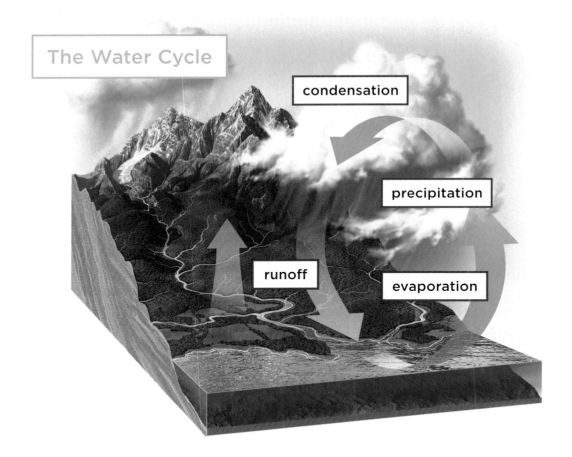

The Water Cycle

condensation

precipitation

runoff

evaporation

As spring turns to summer, hotter temperatures cause liquid water to evaporate, lowering the level of water in the pond. As summer turns to fall, cooler temperatures cause water vapor to condense into liquid water. The process of water vapor changing to liquid water is called **condensation** (kon•den•SAY•shuhn).

Water changes state from gas to liquid to solid when heat is taken away from water. When heat is added to water, the reverse happens, and water changes state from solid to liquid and from liquid to gas.

Water on Earth is never lost. It changes form and moves from place to place in a process called the water cycle. **The water cycle** is the continuous movement of water between Earth's surface and the air as it changes from liquid to gas to solid to liquid.

Water vapor evaporates from the ocean and condenses into clouds. **Fog** is a cloud that forms near the ground. Water falls as **precipitation** (pri•ci•puh•TAY•shuhn) and runs to the ocean. **Precipitation** is water that falls from the air to the ground as rain, sleet, hail, or snow. In the ocean, it evaporates again.

What's With the Weather?

Global warming and a natural shift in weather patterns are causing extreme weather around the globe.

There's not much snow for these skiers in Massachusetts.

W hat's going on? Winter weather comes late in some parts of the country. In other places, bitter cold is an unwelcome surprise. Unusual springlike temperatures are blown away by massive storms. Arctic blasts carry rain, ice, and snow, causing deaths.

Topsy-Turvy Weather

The U.S. recently recorded its warmest year on record. As part of the trend, New York City hit a record-breaking 72°F in early January, while severe cold battered the West Coast. Seattle, Washington, set a 10-year record for consecutive days with snow on the ground. Two big blizzards dumped more than three feet of snow on Colorado, Nebraska, Kansas, and Oklahoma. Freezing temperatures destroyed $1 billion worth of California's citrus crops.

Scientists think global warming is responsible for some of the warmer winter weather. But a natural shift in weather patterns, called El Niño, is also affecting the storms.

▲ Freezing temperatures ruin California citrus crops.

El Niño Events

El Niño events start with rising water temperatures in the Pacific Ocean. The rise in temperature disrupts ocean currents. It affects wind patterns. This combination of changes affects weather around the world. El Niño changes normal rainfall patterns. It can cause severe flooding and severe drought. El Niño events typically last a couple of years. Often an El Niño event is followed by a cooling trend in the Pacific Ocean. This is known as La Niña. La Niña also has severe effects on weather around the world. —*Andrea Delbanco with Susan Moger*

El Niño Effects

El Niño is a natural climate shift. It warms the waters of the Pacific Ocean, which disturbs the flow of winds from their usual east-to-west pattern.

El Niño's effects can vary in strength, but the change always has some impact on weather patterns around the world.

Time For Kids

Predicting Future Weather—NOAA

Have you ever heard the saying, "Everybody talks about the weather, but nobody does anything about it"? Well, the National Oceanographic and Atmospheric Administration (NOAA) is doing something. NOAA's U.S. Seasonal Outlook provides regions of the U.S. with advance weather information. The predictions are based on studies of El Niño and on other sources.

Outlook predicts temperatures and rainfall up to a year in advance. It answers questions such as, Will it be wetter or drier than normal? Will temperatures be above or below average? These long-range predictions benefit farmers. They are also useful for the tourism, transportation, and utilities industries.

But even scientific predictions can be wrong. To update another old saying about weather: "We'll weather the weather, whatever the weather, whether it was predicted or not!"

57

Description Writing Frame

Use the Writing Frame below to orally summarize "Changing States of Water."

Water has many interesting **characteristics**, or states.

One characteristic of water is that it is a _____

_____ .

For example _____
is water in a liquid state.

Another interesting characteristic of water is that it can be

_____ **such as** a _____ .

The water you breathe out with each breath is _____

_____ .

Because of these characteristics, water changes form and _____

_____

_____ .

Use the frame to write the summary on another sheet of paper.
Be sure to include the **bold** signal words. Keep this as a model of
this Text Structure.

Critical Thinking

1 Condensation is the process of _____.

   A. water vapor changing to liquid water

   B. liquid water changing to solid water

   C. liquid water changing to water vapor

2 Find the process in "Changing States of Water" that explains the water cycle.

3 Point to the place in the text "What's With the Weather" that discusses the events of El Niño.

4 Look at the map on page 57. Discuss with a partner how the information helps you understand the article.

The colors used on physical maps include brown or green for land and blue for water.

Digital Learning

For a list of links and activities that relate to this Science standard, visit the California Treasures Web site at www.macmillanmh.com to access the Content Readers resources.

Have children view the e-Review "The Water Cycle."

EL In addition, distribute copies of the Translated Concept Summaries in Spanish, Chinese, Hmong, Khmer, and Vietnamese.

Fresh Water Resources

Only about 1% of Earth's surface is covered by fresh water. Most of this water is in ice sheets and glaciers. Ice sheets and glaciers are usually far from cities and towns, so the fresh water in them is not available to most people. Most of the fresh water that people use for drinking, washing, and cooking is obtained from running water, standing water, and groundwater.

If you look at a map, you may notice that many cities and towns are built next to streams, rivers, or other sources of running water. People build near fresh water because they need a steady source of fresh water for their homes, farms, and businesses.

Lakes, ponds, and reservoirs (RE•zuh•vwahrz) are examples of standing fresh water. These bodies of water fill holes in the ground.

Lakes usually fill deep holes. Ponds are much smaller and shallower than lakes. Their smaller size means they are often not reliable sources of fresh water for people to use.

A **reservoir** is a man-made lake that is used to store water. Reservoirs are usually made by building a dam across a stream or a river. Water builds up behind the dam and is stored there until it is needed. At many reservoirs, activities such as swimming and boating are restricted so the water supply can remain clean.

The water stored behind reservoirs is measured in acre-feet. One acre-foot is a unit of volume that is defined as the volume of water necessary to cover one acre of surface area to a depth of one foot. It is equal to about the amount of water used annually by a family of four.

Usable Fresh Water Sources

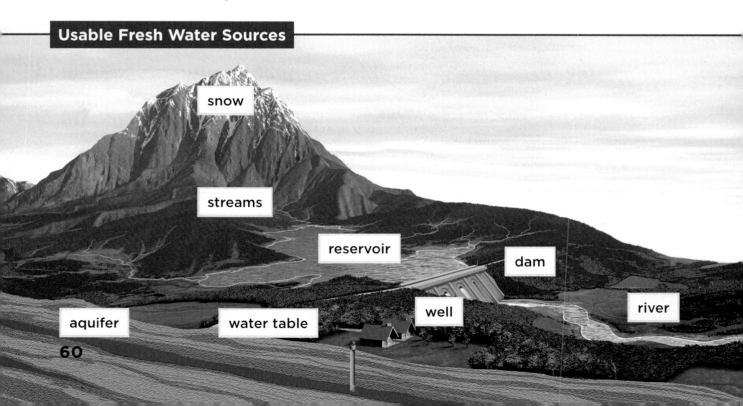

snow

streams

reservoir

dam

well

river

aquifer

water table

60

A water treatment plant in Oakland, California

Communities, homes, farms, and factories that are far from running or standing freshwater sources can get fresh water from groundwater. **Groundwater** is water beneath Earth's surface. Groundwater seeps into the ground through aquifers (A•kwuh•fuhrz). An **aquifer** is an underground layer of rock or soil that is capable of absorbing water. As it seeps down through the ground, water eventually runs into a layer of rock that does not absorb water. Then the fresh water collects there and builds up, forming a water table.

The level of a water table changes as water seeps down from the surface and is removed. Aquifers fill over a period of years. When water is removed from the aquifer, the aquifer requires time to refill. Groundwater is most useful to people when it is close enough to the surface that it is easy to reach by drilling or digging wells into the ground.

The water that flows to houses and businesses in your community is treated, or cleaned, in a water treatment plant. There, fresh water from a lake or reservoir runs though several tanks. In each tank, a different step takes place. The steps may vary depending on the quality of the source of water.

First sticky particles are added to the water to attract any dirt in it. This step is called coagulation. In the next tank, sedimentation takes place. This is when the heavy clumps of dirt and sticky particles fall to the bottom of the tank. Then the water passes through a series of filters, which are layers of sand, gravel, and charcoal. These filters remove any remaining bits of soil or other particles. After water leaves this tank, chemicals such as chlorine are added to the water to kill harmful bacteria. This step is called disinfection. Finally the clean water is stored in a tank or storage area before it flows to the community.

Much Too Dry

A long period without enough rain is causing serious problems in parts of the U.S.

Shriveled, earless stalks of corn. Shrinking watering holes. Dusty, empty pastures where cattle once grazed. This is what severe drought looks like in the Great Plains states. At a time when farmers should be harvesting crops and adding up profits, they count their losses. When grass won't grow on grazing lands, some ranchers have to sell off their cattle.

What Causes Drought?

Drought occurs gradually. First a region gets less rain and snow than usual. Eventually water supplies can't make up for the shortage. Less rain means the soil dries up and plants die. Water levels in rivers and lakes fall. Rain, when it comes, provides some relief. But drought is caused by more than a lack of rainfall. In the states suffering from drought, several years of dry conditions are made worse by winters with little snow. Lack of snow robs the soil of precious moisture reserves. Record heat is the final straw.

Drought means farmers like this one won't have crops to harvest.

Jill Johnson/KRT/NewsCom

An abandoned farm on the Great Plains during the 1930s drought called the Dust Bowl.

Devastating Droughts

In the 1930s terrible droughts hit the Great Plains states. That time is known as the Dust Bowl. Millions of acres of farmland dried up and turned to dust. With no relief in sight, hundreds of thousands of people packed up and left their homes.

Fifty years later came the worst drought since the Dust Bowl. In 1988, after four years of diminished rainfall, drought hit 35 states. The Midwest, the Northern Plains, and the Rockies were hit hard. Rainfall was 85% below normal in some places. The drought killed crops and livestock and fueled forest fires. —*Kathryn Satterfield with Susan Moger*

The Bismarck Tribune

▲ **Cattle in a drought-stricken pasture**

How Dry Is Your State?

Parts of United States are suffering from an extended drought right now. You can find out how wet or dry your state is compared to other states. Check out the web site of the National Climatic Data Center of the U.S. Department of Commerce at **www.ncdc.noaa.gov/oa/climate/research/2007/mar/us-drought.html#StateTables**

Library of Congress

Cause/Effect Writing Frame

Use the Writing Frame below to orally summarize "Much Too Dry."

Droughts have **several causes**. **One reason** droughts occur is

_____

_____ .

When this happens, **the effect is** _____

_____ .

Another cause of droughts is _____

_____ .

Because of this _____

_____ .

Record _____
is **another cause** of drought.

All of these **causes** can lead to severe droughts.

Use the frame to write the summary on another sheet of paper.
Be sure to include the **bold** signal words. Keep this as a model of
this Text Structure.

Critical Thinking

1 An aquifer is _____ .

    A. a man-made lake

    B. water beneath Earth's surface

    C. rock or soil that absorbs water

2 Locate the text in "Much Too Dry" that describes a drought.

3 Point to the sentence in "Fresh Water Resources" where it discusses ice sheets and glaciers.

4 Look at the diagram on page 60. Discuss with a partner the purpose of the diagram.

Diagrams contain labels making it easy to read and remember.

Digital Learning

For a list of links and activities that relate to this Science standard, visit the California Treasures Web site at www.macmillanmh.com to access the Content Readers resources.

Have children view the e-Review "Freshwater Resources."

EL In addition, distribute copies of the Translated Concept Summaries in Spanish, Chinese, Hmong, Khmer, and Vietnamese.

Air Movements

During the day, land heats up faster than water. Air over the land becomes warmer than air over the sea. As it warms, the air over the land becomes less dense and the atmospheric pressure decreases. The column of air over the ocean now has a higher pressure than the column of air over the land. The air over the ocean moves toward the land.

Overnight the land cools off faster than the water. This means that the air over the ocean is warmer and has a lower pressure than the column of air over the land. Air moves from where the pressure is higher to where the pressure is lower. When you stand on the beach and face the ocean in the morning, cool air moves from the land behind you toward the ocean in front of you.

As land and water temperatures change throughout the day, the changing temperatures cause differences in air pressure. Air flows from areas of high pressure to areas of low pressure. As the air flows, it moves heat from one place to another. **Convection** (con•VEK•shuhn) is the transfer of heat through the movement of gas or a liquid. When convection happens in air, it forms winds. Winds can be local breezes or gusts that blow around the world.

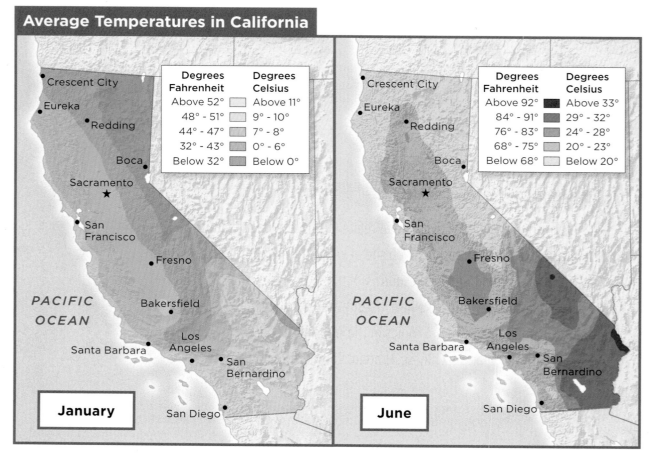

Average Temperatures in California

Degrees Fahrenheit		Degrees Celsius
Above 52°		Above 11°
48° - 51°		9° - 10°
44° - 47°		7° - 8°
32° - 43°		0° - 6°
Below 32°		Below 0°

Crescent City
Eureka
Redding
Boca
Sacramento ★
San Francisco
Fresno
PACIFIC OCEAN
Bakersfield
Los Angeles
Santa Barbara
San Bernardino
San Diego

January

Degrees Fahrenheit		Degrees Celsius
Above 92°		Above 33°
84° - 91°		29° - 32°
76° - 83°		24° - 28°
68° - 75°		20° - 23°
Below 68°		Below 20°

Crescent City
Eureka
Redding
Boca
Sacramento ★
San Francisco
Fresno
PACIFIC OCEAN
Bakersfield
Los Angeles
Santa Barbara
San Bernardino
San Diego

June

What causes temperatures along the coast to be lower in the summer and higher in the winter? Water and land heat the air above them. Air that is in contact with water is tempered, or warmed in the winter and cooled in the summer.

On a summer day the ocean water may have a temperature of 20°C (68°F). The air above the water will be near 20°C. The air temperature will not increase much during the day because the water temperature under it will not increase much.

However, on that same summer day, sunlight warms the land very rapidly. Air above the land will get hotter. Air temperatures may jump 10°F or more in just a few hours.

On a very hot day the temperature of the air above the land may soar to 30°C (86°F). You would feel cooler near the ocean than even a few kilometers inland.

Over the summer the temperature of the water increases slightly as it is warmed by heat energy from the sunlight. The temperature of the oceans does not change much from day to night or from season to season.

In winter the reverse happens. During the fall and winter, the ocean slowly gives up the heat it gained during the summer. By February it may have cooled to 10°C (50°F). However, the land has cooled faster. Its temperature may now be 0°C (32°F). In winter the air over the water usually stays warmer than the air over the land.

Oceans moderate temperatures throughout the year both locally and over the entire planet. The climate of a place near the ocean is more mild than a place inland. **Climate** (KLIGH•muht) is the average weather conditions of a place or region. Climate includes average temperatures, average rainfall, humidity, and wind conditions.

Differences between the temperatures near the equator and those near the poles would be much greater if Earth had no oceans. The slow warming and cooling of the oceans around the world keeps air in a narrow range of temperatures.

Welcome to the Worst Weather in the World

A trip to the top of this mountain can be a thrill or a dangerous encounter with cold and wind.

Mount Washington, in the White Mountains of New Hampshire, isn't the tallest peak in the United States. It isn't even the hardest to climb. You don't have to climb it anyway, because there's a cog railway that runs all the way up to the top. Or you can drive up in a car.

Mount Washington is famous, though, for its weather. Mount Washington boasts the worst weather in the world. Storms blow up without warning. Hikers can die of the cold, even in summer. The highest wind speed ever recorded on Earth was clocked here, in 1934. The wind was blowing at an almost unbelievable 231 miles per hour—much, much faster than the strongest hurricane!

It may sound surprising that a not-very-tall (6,288 feet) mountain in New Hampshire could possibly have such terrible weather. How could it be colder than the North Pole, windier than the South Pole, and stormier than Tornado Alley? It's just luck.

Snow-covered Mount Washington looms over this New Hampshire hotel. ▶

Charles Krebs/Corbis

In the Path of the Storms

Winds usually blow storms along the same routes from west to east. The routes of storms as they move across the United States all come together in New Hampshire.

Once they reach New Hampshire, the storms hit the White Mountains. While the winds blow west to east, the mountain range stretches more or less north to south. The winds hit the solid wall of peaks, then stream up and over the top. As they rise, the winds speed up.

As the winds get faster, they're also squeezed between the mountains. It's like a stream of water rocketing through a narrow nozzle on a hose. And just for a little extra oomph, two spurs of the mountain range angle off in just the right way to steer everything toward Mount Washington. A calm day up here is almost unheard of.

Studying the Weather Where It Lives

The Mount Washington Observatory is a private scientific institution. Its job is to increase our understanding of the natural systems that create Earth's weather and climate. To do this, it conducts weather research, runs educational programs, and studies cosmic rays.

▲ Ice and snow coat the buildings and equipment atop Mount Washington.

Members who pay to be part of the observatory can take part in weather research. They can also come up to the top of the mountain for special programs. —*Lisa Jo Rudy*

Mount Washington Extremes

- The coldest day on Mount Washington is as cold as winter in Antarctica: –120°F.

- The world's highest wind speed was clocked on Mount Washington at 231 miles per hour.

- Some winters, the snowfall reaches 566 inches. Even in May, 100 inches of snow is not unusual.

- Buildings at the top of the mountain are often covered in rime ice—sideways icicles that form when supercooled fog hits and freezes on contact.

- Over 100 people have died on the mountain, mostly of the cold. Others have died in avalanches or from drowning.

Cause/Effect Writing Frame

Use the Writing Frame below to orally summarize "Air Movements."

What **causes** the air to move? During the day, land heats up faster

than water. This **causes** _____.

The result is that the air over the ocean _____.

Overnight the land cools off faster than the water. The **result** is

_____

_____

Land and water temperatures changing throughout the day **cause**

_____ **because** air flows _____.

When this happens the **effect** is the air flow _____.

The transfer of heat through the movement of gas or liquid is _____

_____

When convection happens in air it **causes** _____.

These winds can be local breezes or gusts that blow around
the world.

Use the frame to write the summary on another sheet of paper.
Be sure to include the **bold** signal words. Keep this as a model of
this Text Structure.

Critical Thinking

1 The average weather conditions of a place or region is called _____ .

    A. convection

    B. climate

    C. temperature

2 Mount Washington boasts the worst weather in the world. Find the place in the text of "Welcome to the Worst Weather in the World" that explains why.

3 Point to the sentence in "Air Movements" that defines the word *tempered*.

4 Review the maps on page 66. How do the keys help you? Discuss with a partner.

Labels on maps identify cities, states, rivers, and other land features.

Digital Learning

For a list of links and activities that relate to this Science standard, visit the California Treasures Web site at www.macmillanmh.com to access the Content Readers resources.

Have children view the e-Review "Oceans and Air Temperature."

EL In addition, distribute copies of the Translated Concept Summaries in Spanish, Chinese, Hmong, Khmer, and Vietnamese.

Air Masses and Fronts

It is a warm and sunny day. Suddenly the temperature drops. Puffy white clouds appear in the western sky. As time passes, the clouds grow taller. The drop in temperature and the change in the clouds indicate that something is happening in the atmosphere.

The air in the atmosphere is not the same all over the United States. Weather is affected by the air mass that is passing through your area. An **air mass** is a large region of air that has a similar temperature and humidity.

Air masses can cover thousand of square kilometers of land and water. Depending on where they form, air masses can be cold, warm, dry, or moist. An air mass that forms above a warm area of water will be warm and humid. An air mass that forms over a cold area of land will be cool and dry.

As air masses move they cause changes in the weather. These changes happen where one air mass meets a different air mass. This meeting place between air masses is called a **front**. This boundary marks the front edge of the oncoming air mass.

What happens when a cold and dry air mass runs into a warm and moist air mass? The cold air, which is dense and heavy, moves under the lighter warm air and pushes it up. As the warm air rises, the moisture in the warm air condenses. Towering clouds form, and storms may follow.

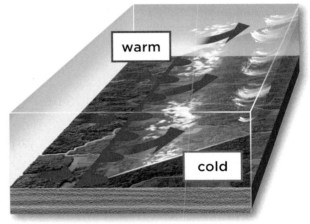

▲ Warm front approaching a cold air mass

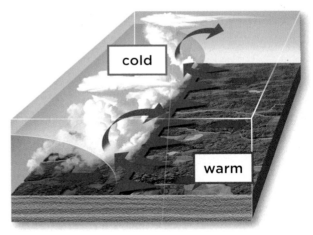

▲ Cold front approaching a warm air mass

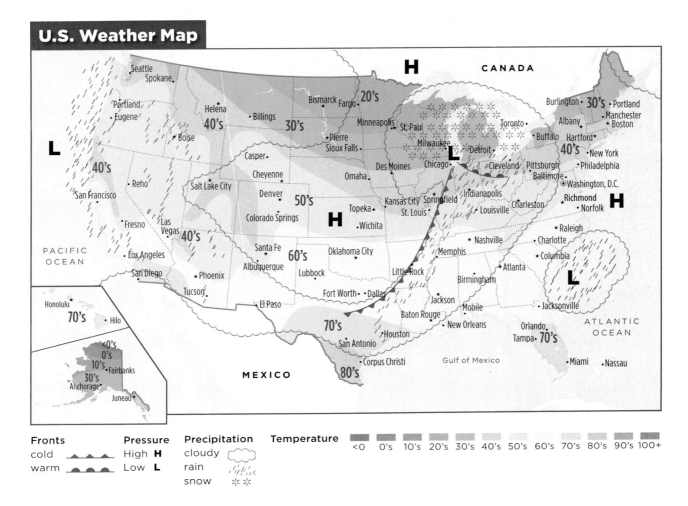

U.S. Weather Map

Fronts
cold
warm

Pressure
High **H**
Low **L**

Precipitation
cloudy
rain
snow

Temperature
<0 0's 10's 20's 30's 40's 50's 60's 70's 80's 90's 100+

To **forecast** (FOR•kast) is to make your best guess before something happens. Meteorologists pay close attention to variables such as wind speed and air pressure so they can improve the accuracy of their predictions.

A **meteorologist** (mee•tee•uh•RAH•luh•jist) is a scientist who specializes in the study of Earth's atmosphere and weather. Meteorologists may predict what the weather will be for the next day, for the next five days, or even for the next few months.

Who needs accurate weather forecasts? Airplane pilots need to know what weather conditions are going to be so they can take off and land safely.

Farmers need to know when rain is coming so they can make sure their crops get enough water.

A weather map shows the weather in a specific area at a specific time. Many different kinds of weather maps exist. They may show only one variable, such as temperature, or they may show many different variables.

The weather map on this page uses symbols to show you cloud cover, air temperature, and precipitation for the United States. If you tracked the weather at your school every day, you could make this kind of weather map.

Around the World in 20 Days

In 1999 two men landed their hot-air balloon in the Egyptian desert and made history.

Fabrice Coffrini/AP Photo

Brian Jones and Bertrand Piccard

Fabrice Coffrini/AP Photo

From Switzerland...

...to Egypt

AP Photo

In March 1999, the Breitling Orbiter 3, a silvery 180-foot-high balloon, circled the world! Bertrand Piccard of Switzerland and Brian Jones of Britain took the balloon on a historic 29,056-mile journey.

Piccard and Jones were the first to go around the world in a balloon. Since 1982 there had been nearly 20 attempts to circle the world in a balloon. All of them failed until the Orbiter 3. Weather experts, technology, good luck, and good winds made it possible.

Hot air balloons fly because of a very basic fact: hotter air is lighter than cooler air. By heating the air that goes into the balloon, balloonists get lift. To lift 1,000 pounds, you need about 65,000 cubic feet of hot air. That's why hot air balloons have to be so big! Piccard and Jones didn't rely on hot air alone. They also used helium, the same gas that is used to make party balloons float.

Inside the Breitling Orbiter 3

Because they planned to fly very high for a long time, Piccard and Jones built a cabin that would become their home away from home. Inside they had all kinds of equipment, including a basic stove, a heater, a toilet, and plenty of freeze-dried food. Along the way, much of their equipment failed, including the heater. Jones said that "although we did have some great views, we had to scrape off the ice before we could see outside."

Making It Around the World

No one can steer a hot-air balloon. The only way to control its direction is to catch the wind going in the direction you want to go. Piccard and Jones knew that they could do this by riding jet streams. Jet streams are fast-moving winds that blow high above the ground, usually from west to east. Balloon pilots go up and down in search of the right wind.

Piccard and Jones took off from Chateau-d'Oex in the Swiss Alps on March 1, 1999. They set down in the Sahara desert in Egypt 20 days later. During its journey, Orbiter 3 crossed China. This was the first balloon to get permission to fly through China's air space.

Bad weather would have meant the end of the expedition. "We were incredibly lucky with the weather—there were storms chasing us over China, for example, but they never caught us up," Jones says.

The annual balloon festival at Chateau-d'Oex

After the Flight

After their historic flight, Piccard and Jones set up a company to encourage other balloonists. They created a special tournament with competitions for balloonists. In 2006, the competition changed. It became an international ballooning festival at Chateau-d'Oex. For one week, people from all over the world come to see thousands of hot air balloons, and, if they're lucky, to take a ride or win a prize.

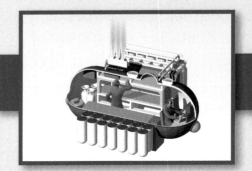

The cabin was well-stocked, but the heater failed.

Description Writing Frame

Use the Writing Frame below to orally summarize "Around the World in 20 Days."

Bertrand Piccard and Brian Jones were the first to go around the world in a balloon. The balloon they used had **many interesting features**.

One interesting feature is that the ballon used hot air and _____

_____.

A second interesting feature is that the balloon had _____

_____.

Inside the cabin _____

_____.

Another interesting feature is that you can not steer a hot-air balloon.

To control the balloon, you have to _____

_____.

Because of these features, Piccard and Jones were able to fly very high for a long time.

Use the frame to write the summary on another sheet of paper. Be sure to include the **bold** signal words. Keep this as a model of this Text Structure.

Critical Thinking

1   A large region of air that has a similar temperature and humidity is called _____ .

    A. forecast

    B. front

    C. air mass

2   How do hot-air balloons fly? Find the paragraph in "Around the World in 20 Days" that provides an answer.

3   Point to the word in "Air Masses and Fronts" for a scientist who specializes in the study of Earth's atmosphere and weather.

4   Look at the diagrams of air masses and fronts on page 72. Discuss with a partner how the information helps you understand the article.

Diagrams help readers see, or visualize, difficult information in a text.

Digital Learning

For a list of links and activities that relate to this Science standard, visit the California Treasures Web site at www.macmillanmh.com to access the Content Readers resources.

Have children view the e-Review "Severe Weather."

EL In addition, distribute copies of the Translated Concept Summaries in Spanish, Chinese, Hmong, Khmer, and Vietnamese.

The Sun

The Sun is a star. A **star** is an object that produces its own energy, including heat and light. Planets and other objects in the solar system that do not produce their own heat and light are not stars.

Stars that produce the most energy make about ten million times more energy than the Sun. The least-productive stars make only one-hundredth as much energy as the Sun.

The Sun is an average-size star and the largest object in the solar system. The Sun's diameter is about 1,390,000 kilometers (863,706 miles). If the Sun were a hollow ball, more than a million Earths could fit inside it. The Sun looks larger than the other stars that can be seen in the night sky because it is much closer to Earth.

The mean, or average, distance between the Sun and Earth is 149,591,000 kilometers (92,960,000 miles). This number is known as one **astronomical** (as•truh•NAH•mi•kulh) **unit** or AU. The closest stars to the solar system are found in the Alpha Centauri star system. They are about 271,931 AUs away.

The Sun is a huge sphere made mostly of two very light gases, hydrogen and helium. About 71% of the Sun's mass is hydrogen. Another 27% is helium. Other materials, such as oxygen and carbon, make up the remaining 2% of the Sun's mass.

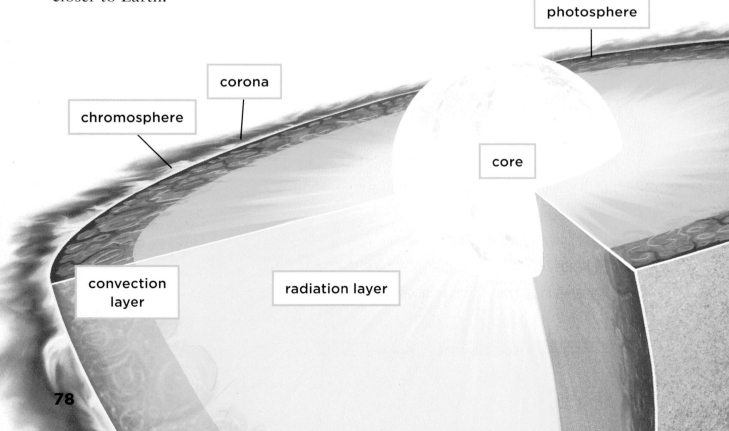

photosphere

corona

chromosphere

core

convection layer

radiation layer

Most of the energy that the Sun produces is formed in its core. At its core, the Sun has a temperature of 10 million to 20 million degrees Celsius. The atmospheric pressure is more than 1 billion times greater than the air pressure at sea level on Earth.

The radiation layer, which is next to the core, moves the energy produced in the core in every direction. It can take millions of years for energy to move out of this layer.

In the convection layer, gases with different energies move in circles in away similar to air with different densities. Energy moves out of this layer in about a week.

The photosphere is the visible surface of the Sun. It is not a solid surface, but rather a layer of gases. The photosphere is cooler than the core. Its temperature is about 5,730°C (10,346°F).

The next layer of the Sun is the chromosphere, or the inner layer of the Sun's atmosphere. When it can be seen, it looks like a red circle around the Sun.

The corona is the outermost layer of the Sun's atmosphere. The corona takes on different shapes around the Sun, depending on changes in the temperature of the photosphere.

Solar flares are bursts of heat and energy that stretch out from the corona and chromospheres into space. Sometimes this energy disrupts satellites, interfering with TV, radio, and cell phone communication systems.

Energy from solar flares also causes displays of different-colored light in the upper atmosphere. These lights are called the *aurora borealis* (uh•ROWR•uh•bawr•ee•AH•luhs), or northern lights. The northern lights are most often seen in Alaska, Canada, and the northern United States. They are only seen in the southern United States when the Sun releases large amounts of energy.

Solar flares are also sometimes associated with sunspots. Sunspots, or dark spots on the Sun, are regions of the photosphere that have a lower temperature than the surrounding regions.

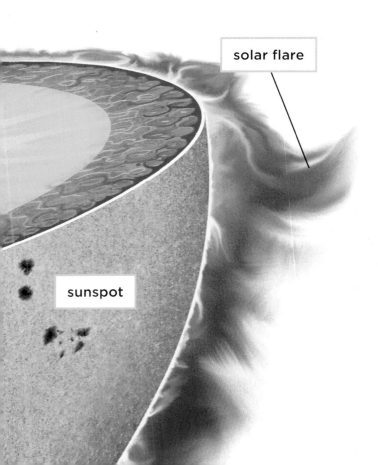

solar flare

sunspot

Looks Like Earth

Astronomers are very interested in a planet that could support life—and it's only 120 trillion miles away.

Is there life beyond planet Earth? To find planets that could be home to some form of life, astronomers observe stars. If they find a telltale wobble in the star's orbit, they can be pretty sure there's a planet nearby causing that wobble.

Planet Hunters

Until recently, astronomers have found evidence only of planets similar to our local planet Jupiter. Based on what we know of Jupiter, none of these planets could possibly support life. After all, Jupiter has no firm surface and no water, and its gravity would smash a person to jelly!

▲ **There are lots of planets like Jupiter, but not many at all like Earth.**

Then, over the past few years, astronomers discovered about 230 planets with more potential for life.

Finally, in 2007, astronomers revealed a new lead in the search for extraterrestrial life. For the first time, they had discovered a planet outside the solar system that could possibly sustain life. The planet, named Gliese 581c, was found by a European telescope located in La Silla, Chile. "It's a significant step on the way to finding possible life in the universe," Michel Mayor says. Mayor was one of the 11 European astronomers on the team that discovered the planet.

The planet was spotted by astronomers at the European Southern Observatory in Chile.

Introducing Gliese 581c

The planet has Earth-like temperatures, even though the star it closely orbits, known as a red dwarf, is much smaller than the Sun. The planet is also about five times as massive as Earth. That means that its gravity would be much greater than Earth's. It would be very tough or even impossible to walk around.

Astronomers do not yet know if there is liquid water on Gliese 581c. "Liquid water is critical to life as we know it," says Xavier Delfosse, an astronomer on the discovery team.

Right in Our Own Cosmic Backyard

Gliese 581c is located 120 trillion miles from Earth, in the constellation Libra. That's only about 20 light-years away—right in our cosmic backyard. "This planet will most probably be a very important target of the future space missions dedicated to the search for extraterrestrial life," says Delfosse. "On the treasure map of the universe, one would be tempted to mark this planet with an X." In this case, the treasure would not be a pirate's chest filled with gold. Instead, it would be some form of life. —*Lisa Jo Rudy*

European Space Observatory/AP Photo

European Space Observatory/AP Photo

A drawing shows the planet in orbit around a red dwarf star (inset).

AFP/Getty Images

The universe may have other planets that support life.

Problem/Solution Writing Frame

Use the Writing Frame below to orally summarize "Looks Like Earth."

Is there life beyond Earth? To solve this **problem**, astronomers

_____ .

Until recently they have found only evidence of planets similar to

Jupiter. **This is a problem because** _____

_____ .

In 2007, astronomers discovered _____

_____ .

Gliese 581c has Earth-like temperatures, however astronomers do
not know if there is life on the planet. **To help solve this problem**

astronomers want to know _____

_____ .

So far **the results are** _____ .

Astronomers will continue their search of Gliese 581c and the rest
of the universe for extraterrestrial life.

• • • • • • • • • • • • • • • • • •

Use the frame to write the summary on another sheet of paper.
Be sure to include the **bold** signal words. Keep this as a model
of this Text Structure.

Critical Thinking

1　An object in the solar system that produces heat and light is a _____ .

   A. sun

   B. star

   C. aura borealis

2　Point to the text in "The Sun" that explains an astronomical unit.

3　Where is Gliese 581c located? Find the text in "Looks Like Earth" that provides an answer.

4　Select a photograph on page 81. With a partner, orally create a new caption for the photograph.

Photographs and captions give visual examples that help explain what the text states.

Digital Learning

For a list of links and activities that relate to this Science standard, visit the California Treasures Web site at www.macmillanmh.com to access the Content Readers resources.

Have children view the e-Review "The Sun."

EL In addition, distribute copies of the Translated Concept Summaries in Spanish, Chinese, Hmong, Khmer, and Vietnamese.

The Solar System

The Sun is at the center of the solar system. The word *solar* means "of the Sun." The **solar system** is a system of objects of, or around, the Sun.

Besides the Sun, the objects in the solar system include the eight planets and their moons. From nearest to farthest from the Sun, the planets are Mercury, Venus, Earth, Mars, Jupiter, Saturn, Uranus, and Neptune. Pluto was downgraded to a dwarf planet in 2006 by the International Astronomical Union.

In 1610 Galileo Galilei used a telescope to observe the planets and saw moons revolving around Jupiter. A **telescope** uses lenses to see distant objects. Before Galileo's discovery, people thought that everything in the solar system revolved around Earth.

Telescopes take pictures of and collect data about objects in the solar system. Scientists have launched some telescopes into space so they can gather data without interference from the Earth's atmosphere. Other telescopes are built on mountains to decrease atmospheric interference.

Scientists analyzing data from a telescope in San Diego County, California, recently found an object that might be a tenth planet. This object, which is called Sedna, was about 90 AU from the Sun.

Space exploration vehicles have examined all of the planets in the solar system except Pluto. The only place explored by astronauts, or people who travel in a space vehicle, is Earth's Moon.

Planetary Data from NASA				
Planet Name	Radius at the Equator (km)	Mean Surface Temperature (°C)	Surface Materials	Rings
Mercury	2,440	179	Rock	No
Venus	6,052	482	Rock	No
Earth	6,378	15	Rock	No
Mars	3,397	−63	Rock	No
Jupiter	71,492	−121	Gas	Yes
Saturn	60,268	−125	Gas	Yes
Uranus	25,559	−193	Gas	Yes
Neptune	24,746	−193 to −153	Gas	Yes
Pluto	1,137	−218	Rock and gas	No

A **moon** is an object that circles around a planet. Different planets have different numbers and sizes of moons.

Moons are also called satellites (SA•tuh•lights). A **satellite** is an object in space that circles around another object. The moons of the planets are natural satellites. Man-made satellites circle around Earth. These provide weather information and are part of communication systems.

When objects in space collide, the impact forms a crater, or a hole. The surface of the Moon has millions of these craters. The craters are easy to see because the impact knocks the surface material away so the darker rock underneath shows through.

Most objects that fall toward Earth burn up in Earth's atmosphere. Since the Moon has no atmosphere, the objects that fall toward it do not burn up. As a result, the Moon has more craters than Earth.

An **asteroid** (AS•tuh•roid) is a rock that revolves around the Sun. Most of the thousands of asteroids in the solar system are located between Mars and Jupiter in the asteroid belt. Many asteroids have irregular shapes, somewhat like a potato. Some asteroids are less than 1 mile wide, while others can be up to 500 miles wide.

A **comet** is a mixture of frozen gases, ice, dust, and rock that moves in an irregular circle around the Sun. When a comet is far from the Sun, it is usually no more than a few kilometers in diameter. However, as it gets closer,

energy from the Sun warms the surface of the comet. This makes the ice melt. Then a glowing ball of gases and dust, which is called a coma, forms around the comet. Once the comet forms, the Sun's energy shapes it into shimmering tails of dust and of gases that may stretch out millions of kilometers into space from the head of the comet.

Because the tails are produced by energy from the Sun, they always blow away from the Sun. Therefore, as a comet moves around the Sun, the comet head always stays closest to the Sun and the tails trail out behind it.

The solar system is full of other small objects. In space, these objects are called **meteoroids** (MEE•tee•uh•roids). The objects that cross paths with Earth and enter Earth's atmosphere are called **meteors** (MEE•tee•uhrs).

▼ Earth's Moon is the only moon that can be seen without using a telescope.

Catch a Comet by Its Tail

NASA

A space capsule captures evidence of cosmic history and brings it back to Earth.

The space capsule blazed through the skies at 30,000 miles per hour. Nearing Earth, it was slowed by parachutes. Then it landed safely in a Utah desert. The capsule was from space mission *Stardust,* and it carried a special cargo. On board was the first material ever collected from a comet.

What Are Comets?

Comets are chunks of ice, rock, and dust that are billions of years old. The comets we see from Earth come from a region called the Kuiper Belt. It is located just outside the orbit of Neptune. These comets orbit the Sun in 200 years or less. When one gets close to the Sun, we can see it from Earth.

Surprising Stardust Images

Stardust took close-up images of the comet Wild 2 (pronounced "vilt") from

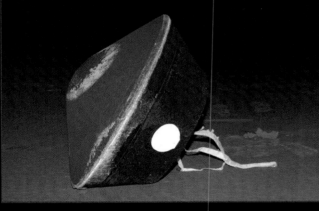

▼ **The Stardust capsule streaked through Earth's atmosphere and landed in the Utah desert.**

NASA

about 150 miles away. The images of the comet's core, "a dirty snowball" made of dust and ice, surprised NASA scientists. "We were amazed by the feature-rich surface of the comet," says Donald Brownlee of the University of Washington. "There are barn-size boulders, 100-meter high cliffs, and some weird terrain unlike anything we've ever seen before."

NASA

Closeup of a comet ▶

36

Precious Particles

Five years after its 1999 launch, *Stardust* flew to within 150 miles of Comet 81P/Wild 2. Stardust stuck out a tennis-racket-like contraption to catch tiny grains of material being blown off the surface of the comet. The microscopic particles were put in aerogel, an airy goo. Aerogel is so light, it has been described as frozen smoke. The aerogel kept the comet particles safe for the trip to Earth.

Why is this so exciting? Comets are like cosmic time capsules. They contain material that has been in the deep freeze for more than 4.5 billion years. By looking at comet particles, scientists can get information about how the solar system formed.

Volunteers at Work

After the particles packed in aerogel arrived on Earth, scientists used a scanning microscope to collect digital images of the aerogel contents. These images were made available to volunteer scientists around the world.

Douglas C. Pizac/ AP Photo

▲ **A researcher retrieves cosmic dust.**

Volunteers had to pass a test given on the *Stardust* mission Web page. One scientist compared the task to searching for ants on a football field. Once particles were located, researchers carefully extracted the dust to analyze it. As a reward, the volunteers who located grains of space dust got to name them!

Something New in the Universe

"A portion of the organic material in the samples is unlike anything seen before," says Scott Sandford, a NASA scientist. "[P]eople will be working on these samples for decades to come," he said. In terms of their scientific value, he continued, the particles are "a gift that keeps on giving."

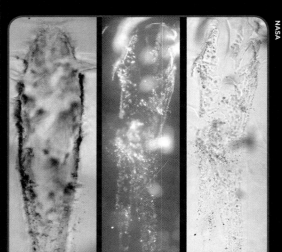

NASA

◀ **Particles of comet dust trapped in aerogel**

Compare/Contrast Writing Frame

Use the Writing Frame below to orally summarize "The Solar System."

A moon or satellite is _____ .

An asteroid is _____ .

A comet is _____ .

They are **all** a part of _____ .

Moons and asteroids **are similar because** _____ .

However, moons and asteroids **are different because** _____

_____ .

Asteroids and comets **are alike because** they both are made of

_____ . In addition **they both** circle

_____ . However, they are **different**

because a comet is also made of _____ .

So, the objects in our solar system have **similarities and differences**.

• • • • • • • • • • • • •

Use the frame to write the summary on another sheet of paper.
Be sure to include the **bold** signal words. Keep this as a model
of this Text Structure.

Critical Thinking

1 What instrument does a scientist use to observe the solar system?

    A. satellite

    B. microscope

    C. telescope

2 Point to the word in "The Solar System" that describes an object in space that circles around another object.

3 Describe what a comet is using text from "Catch a Comet by Its Tail."

4 Review the chart on page 84. Do any of the planets have rings? Share with a partner how you located the answer.

> Charts may show different categories to help the reader organize information.

Digital Learning

For a list of links and activities that relate to this Science standard, visit the California Treasures Web site at www.macmillanmh.com to access the Content Readers resources.

Have children view the e-Review "The Structure of the Solar System."

EL In addition, distribute copies of the Translated Concept Summaries in Spanish, Chinese, Hmong, Khmer, and Vietnamese.

Gravity

Each planet in the solar system is drawn toward the Sun by gravity. **Gravity** is a force of attraction, or pull, between any two objects. The strength of the pull of gravity is different between different pairs of objects. Gravity is affected by the total mass of the two objects. It is also affected by the distances between the objects.

All objects have mass and all objects are pulled toward one another by gravity. However, the strength of the pull, or gravity, decreases when the total mass of the two objects decreases.

Gravity is a force that acts over a distance. Two objects do not have to touch each other to produce a force of gravity between them. The strength of gravity depends on how far apart the objects are. The pull gets weaker when the objects are farther apart.

The pull of gravity between Earth and the Sun acts across about 150 million kilometers of space. Gravity also acts across roughly 6 billion kilometers of space between the Sun and Pluto. Since the distance is farther between the Sun and Pluto, the pull of gravity between the Sun and Pluto is weaker than the pull of gravity between the Sun and Earth.

An **orbit** is a path one object takes around another object. Planets orbit the Sun, and moons orbit their planets. Planets are held in their orbits by the force of gravity between each planet and the Sun.

Astronaut John Young can jump higher on the Moon than on Earth because the Moon's gravity is about $\frac{1}{6}$ of Earth's gravity.

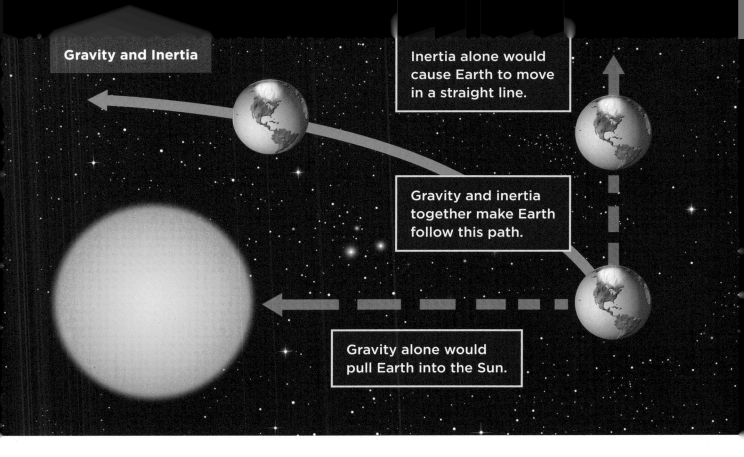

Gravity and Inertia

Inertia alone would cause Earth to move in a straight line.

Gravity and inertia together make Earth follow this path.

Gravity alone would pull Earth into the Sun.

If gravity was the only force acting on a planet, the planet would be pulled into the Sun. What prevents this from happening? All objects have a property called inertia (I•nur•shuh). **Inertia** is the tendency of a moving object to keep moving in a straight line.

As a space vehicle orbits Earth, members of the crew float in the cabin. They are weightless. Why aren't the crew or other objects inside the space vehicle being pulled toward Earth by gravity?

Like all objects in an orbit, the pull of gravity on the space vehicle is balanced by its forward motion. If the space vehicle sped up, its forward motion would overcome the pull of Earth's gravity. The vehicle would pull out of that orbit and move further away from Earth.

Planets in the solar system act much like the space vehicle. As the planets orbit the Sun, they tend to fall toward it. But at the same time, their forward motion tends to make them move away from it.

The effect of these two motions makes the planets move in a nearly circular orbit called an ellipse (i•LIPS). When the Earth is closest to the Sun, it is 147,098,074 kilometers away. When Earth is furthest from the Sun, it is 152,097,701 kilometers away. This 5 million kilometer difference shows that Earth's orbit is an ellipse and not a perfect circle.

To Pluto...
and Beyond!

The *New Horizons* spacecraft is on its way to Pluto, and it's doing a lot of sightseeing along the way.

NASA launched its first mission to Pluto and beyond in January 2006. The 1,000-pound *New Horizons* spacecraft passed Jupiter in February 2007. It will reach Pluto and its moons, Charon, Nix, and Hydra, in July 2015. Then the spacecraft will head deeper into space.

New Horizons is the fastest spacecraft ever, traveling nearly 10 miles per second. At that speed, it could travel from New York to Kansas in just two minutes. It raced past the Moon in nine hours and Jupiter in 13 months.

Pluto, made of rock and ice, was once considered to be the ninth planet in our solar system. Recently, however, Pluto lost its status as a planet. Even though it's no longer a planet, Pluto is still extremely interesting to scientists. "[Pluto] is now central to our understanding of the origin of our solar system," says Alan Stern, lead mission scientist.

Frozen Mini-Worlds

Pluto is one of thousands of icy space chunks located in a area known as the Kuiper (KY•puhr) Belt. The Kuiper Belt lies in a dark, frigid zone 3 billion to 5 billion miles from the Sun.

▲ The *New Horizons* scacecraft is readied for launch.

▼ A powerful Atlas rocket carries *New Horizons* into space.

These worlds have been in a deep freeze since the solar system formed more than 4 billion years ago. For that reason, they are a frozen record of what conditions were like then.

Those ancient conditions are what Stern and his colleagues will try to understand when *New Horizons* reaches Pluto and its three moons in 2015. As the probe zips by, its cameras will snap pictures of the surface, analyze Pluto's thin atmosphere, and take its temperature.

▲ The *New Horizons* probe is the size of a grand piano.

Along the Way

New Horizons has already sent back interesting information about the solar system. It came to within 1.4 million miles of Jupiter in February 2007. For several weeks before and after this closest approach, the robotic probe used its sensors and seven cameras to explore Jupiter and its four largest moons. Jupiter was a good first test of *New Horizon's* ability to operate on its own.

Prepare to Be Surprised

For many years it was easy to think of the solar system as nine lonely worlds traveling in neat rings around the Sun. But the harder astronomers look beyond Pluto, the more crowded our cosmic neighborhood seems to become. —*Michael D. Lemonick*

▲ On its way to Pluto, *New Horizons* photographed Jupiter and its moon, Io.

Description Writing Frame

Use the Writing Frame below to orally summarize "To Pluto...and Beyond!"

The *New Horizons* spacecraft has **many interesting features**.

One interesting feature is that the spacecraft weighs _____

_____ .

A second interesting feature is *New Horizons* _____

_____ .

It raced past the Moon in nine hours and Jupiter in 13 months.

Another interesting feature is the robotic probe. This probe has

_____

_____ .

Because of these features *New Horizons* will reach Pluto and its three moons in 2015 and help scientists learn more about the solar system.

Use the frame to write the summary on another sheet of paper. Be sure to include the **bold** signal words. Keep this as a model of this Text Structure.

Critical Thinking

1   The tendency of a moving object to keep moving in a straight line is called _____.

   A. inertia

   B. orbit

   C. gravity

2   What is gravity affected by? Locate the text in "Gravity" that provides an answer.

3   Point to the word in "To Pluto...and Beyond!" for icy space chunks located in an area known as the Kuiper Belt.

4   How do the arrows help you understand the diagram on page 91?

Pay attention to the arrows in diagrams. They show the direction in which something moves.

Digital Learning

For a list of links and activities that relate to this Science standard, visit the California Treasures Web site at www.macmillanmh.com to access the Content Readers resources.

Have children view the e-Review *"Gravity and Orbit."*

EL In addition, distribute copies of the Translated Concept Summaries in Spanish, Chinese, Hmong, Khmer, and Vietnamese.

A VARIED LAND

Over thousands of years, many Native American groups in North America developed unique cultures with different traditions and ways of life. From the freezing cold of the Arctic of northern Alaska to the dry desert heat of the Southwest, Native American lives varied as much as the landscape of the United States.

The story of Native Americans is usually divided into two parts. The first part is called **Pre-Columbian** because it takes place before Columbus arrived in 1492. The second part is after Columbus and Europeans arrived in North America.

The Arctic is one of Earth's harshest environments. Yet the Inuit (I•noo•wuht) have lived there for more than 2,000 years. They settled in what are today northern and northwestern Alaska, Canada, and Greenland. The Inuit also live in Siberia in Russia.

Arctic winters are dark and cold, while summers are sunny and mild. The Inuit who settled in the Arctic had to find ways to live through changing seasons.

In the winter, Inuit men built houses that were partially underground and were made of soil and wood. When they traveled to hunt, men built igloo homes made of large snow blocks.

In the warmer weather, they made tents from wooden poles and animal skins. When men returned from hunting, women cooked the meat and made warm clothing from the skin. Walruses, seals, fish, and whales provided materials for weapons, tools and food as well as oil for lighting and cooking.

In contrast, east of the Mississippi River, giant forest cover the land. The trees, plants, and animals of the forest provided everything the people needed to survive.

In the 1500s the Iroquois lived mostly in what is now upstate New York. Historians call this group Iroquois because they spoke languages in the Iroquoian language family. However, the Iroquois call themselves Hodenosaunee (how•den•NO•sah•nee). In Iroquoian this means "people of the longhouse." **Longhouses** are long buildings made of poles covered with sheets of bark.

Iroquois men built houses, hunted, fished, and were responsible for fighting. Iroquois women took care of gathering food, cooking, and housekeeping. Iroquois women also decided how the land would be used, and who would use it. They were the leaders of their clans. A **clan** is group of families who share the same ancestor.

Almost all Iroquois property was controlled by clans. Women were the owners of the land and the longhouses. When a man married, he moved into his wife's longhouse and lived with her family. Children took their clan name from their mother. The head of each clan was called a clan mother. No important decision could be made without the approval of the clan mother. Although the leaders of each village were men, it was the clan mothers who chose them.

In about 1570, five separate Iroquois peoples joined together to form the **Iroquois Confederacy**, also know as the Iroquois League.

To help keep peace among the nations, the Iroquois people developed the Great Law, which is a set of rules for the Iroquois people. The Grand Council was also established to maintain peace. The clan mothers of each nation sent representatives to the council. The council made decisions through discussion and compromise. A **compromise** is the settling of a dispute by each side agreeing to give up part of what it wants. Some historians believe the Great Law may have influenced the plan of the American government. The Grand Council continues to make decisions for the Iroquois today.

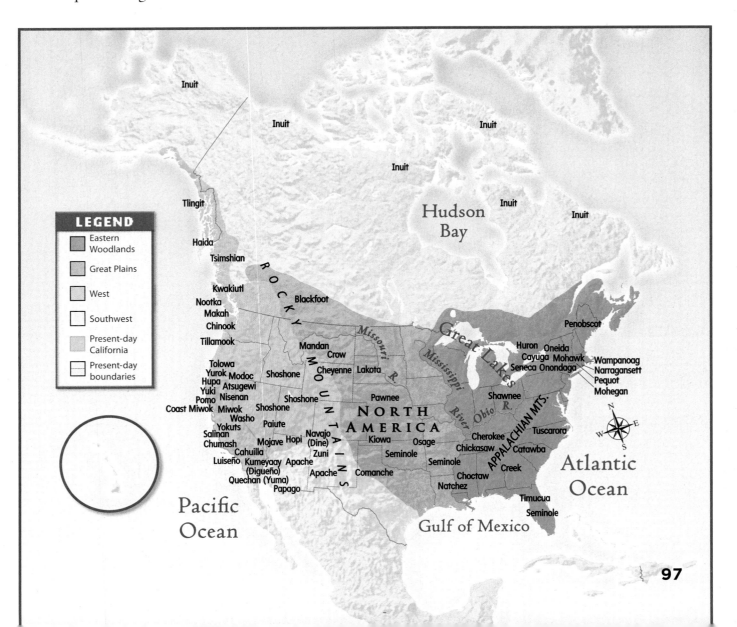

Who Were the First Americans?

An ancient skeleton helps modern scientists answer some old questions.

For decades scientists believed that the earliest Americans came from Asia about 12,000 years ago. They thought that ancient people walked across dry land that connected what is now Russia and Alaska. But new discoveries are causing scientists to take another look at this idea.

Kennewick Man

In 1996 two college students were digging on the bank of the Columbia River, near Kennewick, Washington. They found a skull that looked ancient. More bones were found later. Scientists ran tests that showed that the skeleton was 9,400 years old!

The skeleton was called Kennewick Man. It is one of the oldest skeletons ever found in the Americas. None of the others were as complete as Kennewick Man. For about nine years Kennewick Man was at the center of an argument. Native Americans wanted the skeleton treated with respect and reburied. Scientists wanted to study the bones. A group of researchers went to court.

ASIA

Kennewick Man

▲ A scientist examines the skull of Kennewick Man

Tim Dillehay

Possible routes for human migration from Asia to North and South America

BERING LAND BRIDGE

Arctic Ocean

LAURENTIDE ICE SHEET

NORTH AMERICA

Ice-free corridor passable about 12,000 years ago

CORDILLERAN ICE SHEET

CANADA

On Your Knees Cave ALASKA 9,818 B.P.

Kennewick WASH. 9,400 years old

Daisy Cave CALIF. 10,500 B.P.

U.S.

Cedros Island MEXICO 11,000 B.P.

MEXICO

Folsom N.M. 10,490 B.P.

Clovis N.M. 11,200 B.P.

Meadowcroft PA. ▲ 14,250 B.P.

Cactus Hill VA. 15,070 B.P.

Topper S.C. ▲ 15,200 B.P.

Select archaeological sites:

● Human remains found   ■ Other artifacts found   ▲ Dates in dispute

B.P. = Before Present

Taima-Taima VENEZUELA 13,000 B.P.

VENEZUELA

Tibitó COLOMBIA 11,740 B.P.

COLOMBIA

Equator

BRAZIL

SOUTH AMERICA

Pedra Furada BRAZIL ▲ 47,000 B.P.

■ Lapa do Boquete BRAZIL Up to 12,070 B.P.

PERU

Quebrada Jaguay PERU 10,500 B.P.

BOLIVIA

CHILE

ARGENTINA

Monte Verde CHILE 12,500 B.P.

Palli Aike CHILE 8,640 B.P.

Who Discovered America?

Kennewick Man is just one of a number of discoveries that have changed ideas about the first people in the Americas. Since the 1980s scientists have made discoveries in Monte Verde, Chile, and Daisy Cave, California, that changed theories about when the first Americans arrived.

Many scientists now think that people arrived in the Americas much earlier than 12,000 years ago. They believe that groups traveled down the Pacific coast of North and South America.

Scientists have also made discoveries in South Carolina. A few believe that early Americans may have come from Europe to the Atlantic Coast.

By studying discoveries like Kennewick Man, they hope to learn more about how people came to the Americas. —*Michael D. Lemonick and Andrea Dorfman*

▼ **An artist's drawing of what Kennewick Man might have looked like**

Raul Colón

Something to Think About

Who should own ancient bones, scientists or the people who own the land where they were found? Why?

TIME FOR KIDS

Compare/Contrast Writing Frame

Use the Writing Frame below to orally summarize "A Varied Land."

When you **compare** the Inuit and Iroquois, you discover that

they **both** have developed _____

_____.

The Inuit settled in what are today _____.

In contrast, the Iroquois _____.

Like the Iroquois, Inuit men _____

_____.

However, **unlike** the Inuit, Iroquois women _____

_____.

Inuit and Iroquois women were **both** responsible for _____

_____.

In **contrast** Iroquois women decided _____

_____.

Use the frame to write the summary on another sheet of paper. Be sure to include the **bold** signal words. Keep this as a model of this Text Structure.

Critical Thinking

1   A building made of poles covered with sheets of bark is called a _____ .

   A. longhouse

   B. clan

   C. igloo

2   Find the sentence in "A Varied Land" that explains what compromise means.

3   Find the paragraph in "Who Were the First Americans?" that describes what Kennewick Man looked like.

4   Study the map on page 99. With a partner, discuss the possible routes Kennewick Man could have traveled to Washington State.

> The legend or key on a map helps you understand the symbols or colors on a map.

Digital Learning

For a list of links and activities that relate to this History/Social Science standard, visit the California Treasures Web site at www.macmillanmh.com to access the Content Readers resources. Have children view the video "Native People of North America."

TRADE AND TRAVEL

About 1,500 years ago, Europe was less advanced in many ways than the civilizations of the Americas. At the time, Europe was an area of small countries, which were often at war with one another. This period of European history is called the **Middle Ages** because it falls between the time of the ancient cultures and the beginnings of the world we live in today.

During the Middle Ages, travel was dangerous and took a long time. As Europeans traveled beyond their borders to sell goods, they spread their ideas to foreigners and learned about other cultures. These **merchants**, people who made a living from buying and selling goods, learned new ideas in science, medicine, and technology and shared them upon their return.

The Middle Ages was also a time of religious change. From 1095 to 1270, European Christians journeyed to Palestine to win control of the Holy Land from Muslims. This was known as the **Crusades**. During the 1400s, Spanish Christians successfully fought to recapture their lands from Moors, Arab followers of the religion of Islam. Spanish call this recapture of territory the **Reconquista**.

In 1517 a German priest named Martin Luther wanted to reform, or change, the way in which the Church worked. Luther and his followers became known as Protestant Christians because they protested against the Roman Catholic Church. This movement is known as the **Protestant Reformation**. The response by the Catholic Church to the criticisms is known as the **Counter Reformation**. These leaders agreed there had to be changes, but they wanted to improve the Catholic Church from within.

▼ **Martin Luther preaches to a group of German Protestants.**

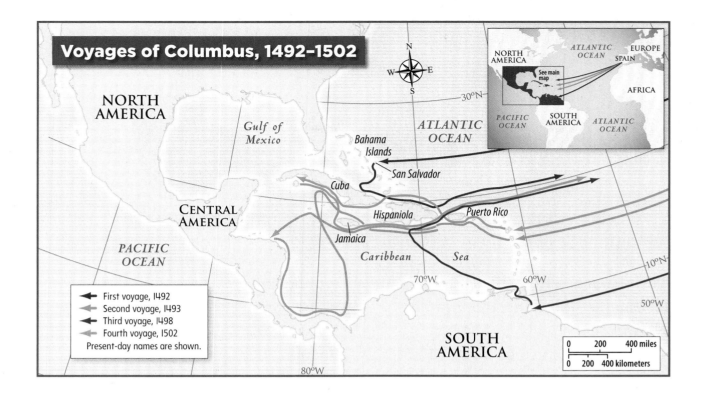

Voyages of Columbus, 1492–1502

NORTH AMERICA

Gulf of Mexico

Bahama Islands

San Salvador

Cuba

ATLANTIC OCEAN

CENTRAL AMERICA

Hispaniola

Puerto Rico

PACIFIC OCEAN

Jamaica

Caribbean   Sea

◄— First voyage, 1492
◄— Second voyage, 1493
◄— Third voyage, 1498
◄— Fourth voyage, 1502
Present-day names are shown.

SOUTH AMERICA

0   200   400 miles
0   200   400 kilometers

NORTH AMERICA   ATLANTIC OCEAN   EUROPE   SPAIN
See main map
PACIFIC OCEAN   SOUTH AMERICA   ATLANTIC OCEAN   AFRICA

The experiences of merchants, combined with the religious change made other Europeans curious about the people beyond the borders of Europe.

By the late 1400s, Europeans knew that the islands of Southeast Asia , which they called the Indies, held great riches, including spices, silk, and gold. However, Portuguese and Mediterranean traders controlled the sea routes around Africa to Asia. This was because in the early 1400s Portugal's Prince Henry had gathered experts to study and improve sailing. They worked on problems of **navigation**— finding direction and following routes at sea by studying mapmaking and using compasses. This information gave the Portuguese a seafaring advantage over other countries.

Other European traders and explorers hoped they would make huge fortunes by finding new, shorter routes to the Indies. Christopher Columbus, a sailor from Genoa, Italy, believed that the fastest way to reach the Indies was to sail west from Europe. He tried for several years to raise money for ships, crews, and supplies. Finally Queen Isabella and King Ferdinand of Spain agreed to pay for his **expedition**. An expedition is a journey made for a special purpose.

After several months at sea, Columbus reached the Bahamas Islands on October 12, 1492. Yet Columbus thought he was near Asia. Because he believed he was in the Indies, Columbus called the local people Indios, which is Spanish for "Indians." We know that the people he saw were a Native American group called the Taíno.

Columbus made three more voyages to the Americas. On his third voyage, he reached the South American mainland for the first time.

The successful expeditions of Columbus encouraged other brave explores to set sail for the Americas.

Explorers and Technology

Gary C. Knapp/AP Photo

Seafaring explorers of the past used technology to guide them in their travels.

▲ **A modern sailor uses high-tech equipment.**

The ocean is a huge place. It has no landmarks—no trees, mountains, rivers, rocks, roads, or houses. Today's sailors use all kinds of technology to figure out where they are and where they're going. Using global positioning systems, cell phones, satellite phones, and radios, they can be sure they're headed in the right direction.

Before the invention of these technologies, though, sailors still crossed the ocean. Some even sailed around the world and found their way home again. How did explorers like Christopher Columbus, Francisco Vásquez de Coronado, James Cook, and Ferdinand Magellan know where they were and where to go?

Unlike most of today's sailors, they used the stars to guide them. Like today's sailors, though, they also used technology. Their technology relied not on electricity, but on mechanics and the laws of physics. —*Lisa Jo Rudy*

Datacraft/Getty Images

Columbus used the stars to find his way to the New World.

Bettmann/Corbis

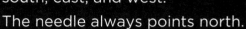

The Astrolabe

Sailors often used the North Star to get their bearings. Even though the North Star (Polaris) is generally in the northern part of the sky, it can be seen only on clear nights. What's more, it can only be seen from certain parts of Earth.

The first tool for celestial navigation—navigation using stars—came from the Middle East. The astrolabe is a tool used to locate and predict the positions of the Sun, Moon, planets, and stars. To use an astrolabe, you need to know quite a bit about astronomy and math.

The Compass

A compass is a free-floating magnetized needle. The needle floats above a circle that shows north, south, east, and west. The needle always points north.

Before the invention of the compass, sailors had to rely on the stars to steer their way. The compass was extremely helpful to sailors in places where the skies were cloudy. No one knows who invented the compass. Some believe it was first used by native people in South and Central America. We know it was used in ancient China because it was described in Chinese writing around 1000 A.D. The compass may have traveled from China to Europe with traders.

The Sextant

The sextant is a measuring instrument. Sailors use it to measure the height of a celestial object (like the Sun or the Moon) above the horizon. The angle, and the time when it is measured, help the sailor to find his position on a nautical chart.

The first sextant was constructed in Iran in 994. It came to Spain in the twelfth century and replaced the astrolabe as the preferred navigation tool for sailors.

Today the sextant, along with the compass, is still used by some sailors as a backup to modern technology.

Description Writing Frame

Use the Writing Frame below to orally summarize "Explorers and Technology."

Christopher Columbus, Francisco Vásquez de Coronado, James Cook, and Ferdinand Magellan used **many interesting tools** to help them sail across the ocean.

One important tool was the astrolabe. The astrolabe is _____

_____ .

To use one, you need to know _____

_____ .

The compass is **another important tool**. A compass

is _____ .

Measuring instruments **such as** the _____

were also important. Sailors used it _____

_____ .

Because of these important tools, explorers were able to travel all over the world!

Use the frame to write the summary on another sheet of paper. Be sure to include the **bold** signal words. Keep this as a model of this Text Structure.

Critical Thinking

1 A journey made for a special purpose is called
a _____ .

    A. crusade

    B. navigation

    C. expedition

2 Find the word in "Explorers and Technology" that tells
what a free-floating magnetized needle is.

3 Point to the paragraph in "Trade and Travel" that
explains the Reformation.

> Captions help the
> reader tell the difference
> between images that
> may seem quite similar
> at first glance.

4 Compare the photos on page 105 of the astrolabe
and the compass. Discuss the similarities and
differences with a partner.

Digital Learning

For a list of links and activities that relate to this History/Social
Science standard, visit the California Treasures Web site at
www.macmillanmh.com to access the Content Readers resources.
Have children view the video "Exploration and Colonization."

EXPLORING THE UNITED STATES

The areas to the north of Spain's colonies in Central America and the Caribbean were still largely **frontier** in the 1500s. Frontier is a word used by colonists for the far edge of an area they have settled. Spanish explorers headed into the frontier, land that would later become the United States. The first was Juan Ponce de León, who reached Florida's Gulf Coast in 1513.

In 1528 a Spanish conquistador named Alvar Nuñez Cabeza de Vaca was sailing west along the Gulf Coast, when a hurricane shipwrecked his boat on the east coast of what is now Texas.

Cabeza de Vaca and his crew lived among Native Americans in Texas for four years. They then left, making their way to Mexico. In 1536 Cabeza de Vaca and his group arrived in Mexico City, after walking through what are now Texas, New Mexico, and Arizona.

In 1538 Hernado de Soto set out on an expedition with an army in search of riches. They traveled nearly 4,000 miles across what is now the Southeast of the United States and became the first Europeans to see the Mississippi River. De Soto became ill and died in 1542. He never found the treasure he was seeking.

In 1542 Portuguese explore Juan Rodríguez Cabrillo led the first European expedition from New Spain north to what is now California. Sixty years later, Sebastian Vinzcaíno claimed California land for Spain and gave names to places that we still use today.

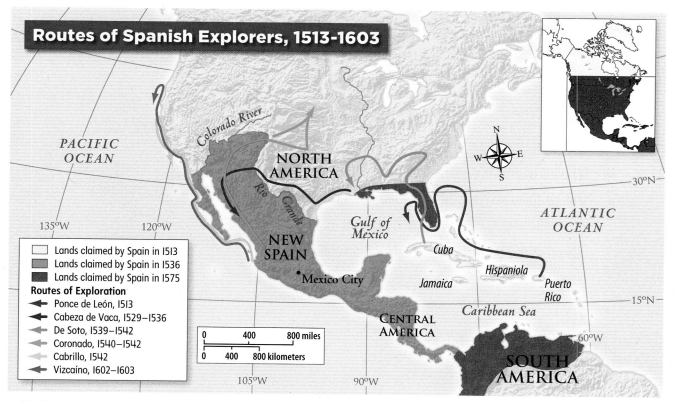

Routes of Spanish Explorers, 1513-1603

PACIFIC OCEAN

Colorado River

NORTH AMERICA

Rio Grande

135°W   120°W

NEW SPAIN

•Mexico City

Gulf of Mexico

Cuba

Jamaica

Hispaniola

Puerto Rico

ATLANTIC OCEAN

30°N

15°N

60°W

Caribbean Sea

Lands claimed by Spain in 1513
Lands claimed by Spain in 1536
Lands claimed by Spain in 1575
Routes of Exploration
Ponce de León, 1513
Cabeza de Vaca, 1529–1536
De Soto, 1539–1542
Coronado, 1540–1542
Cabrillo, 1542
Vizcaíno, 1602–1603

0   400   800 miles
0   400   800 kilometers

CENTRAL AMERICA

SOUTH AMERICA

105°W   90°W

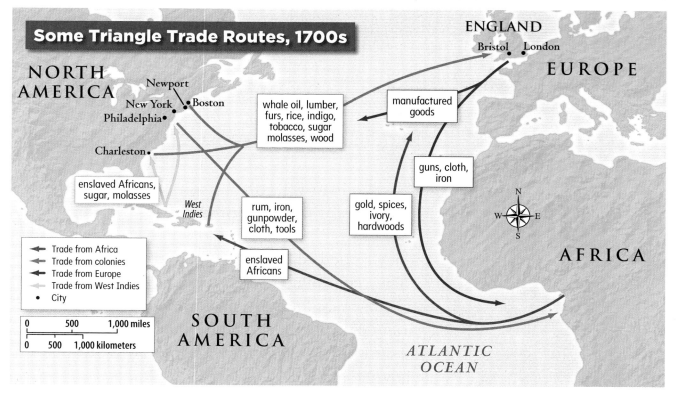

Some Triangle Trade Routes, 1700s

NORTH AMERICA

Newport
New York • Boston
Philadelphia •

Charleston •

whale oil, lumber, furs, rice, indigo, tobacco, sugar molasses, wood

enslaved Africans, sugar, molasses

West Indies

rum, iron, gunpowder, cloth, tools

enslaved Africans

ENGLAND
Bristol London

EUROPE

manufactured goods

guns, cloth, iron

gold, spices, ivory, hardwoods

AFRICA

Trade from Africa
Trade from colonies
Trade from Europe
Trade from West Indies
• City

0   500   1,000 miles
0   500   1,000 kilometers

SOUTH AMERICA

ATLANTIC OCEAN

▲ The English colonies traded with England and Africa. This was one of the routes called the triangular trade because its ocean routes formed triangles.

While the Spanish explored land in the west, Europeans were searching for a shortcut, called the **Northwest Passage**, to Asia. This water route was believed to flow through North America to Asia, connecting the Atlantic and Pacific Oceans.

The English, French, and Dutch hired explores such as John Cabot, Giovanni de Verrazano, and Henry Hudson to search for this route. None of their expeditions found the Northwest Passage, but they did lead to the development of New France, New Netherlands, New Sweden, and the English Colonies.

As the English colonies developed, they began to compete with England for **triangular trade**. Until the late 1600s, England had been able to control most trade with Africa and the West Indies. This created great profits for England. Shipowners wanted their boats to carry cargo on every voyage because selling it

covered the cost of the voyage. Triangular trade was designed to sell products and pick up cargo at each stop.

On the first leg of the route, traders sailed from New England to Africa with manufactured goods, including guns, gunpowder, rum, and cloth. These goods were traded for African captives.

On the second leg of the route, the traders took the African captives to the West Indies. This leg of the route was called the Middle Passage, because it was the middle part of the three-sided trade. In the West Indies, the Africans were sold into slavery. The ship's captains brought molasses, or thick syrup made from sugarcane grown in the Caribbean islands.

On the third leg, the traders transported the molasses to a port in the Northern Colonies. The molasses was sold and made into rum. Then the trade began again.

The Taíno World: Contact and Impact

A rich Caribbean culture was nearly wiped out by European explorers and settlers.

They settled islands throughout the Caribbean. They controlled long-distance trade routes. They were fishermen, hunters, and farmers. They created a variety of sophisticated tools, musical instruments and pottery. Then they met European explorers and died by the millions. They were the Taíno.

A Vanished Way of Life

In 1492 the Taíno (tie•EE•no) culture was the most highly developed in the Caribbean. These creative people lived in island countries we now call Cuba, Puerto Rico, Jamaica, the Bahamas, Haiti, and the Dominican Republic.

Taíno farmers cultivated pineapple, guava, and papaya. They also grew squash, beans, peppers, tobacco, and cotton. The Taíno built huge canoes for fishing and long-distance trading. Some of the canoes could hold 100 people.

The Taíno made wooden spears and household items. They also made musical instruments.

The Granger Collection

The Taíno greet Columbus in what is now called Cuba.

Taíno art on the wall of a cave in the Dominican Republic

Tomas Van Houtryve/AP Photo

Jay I. Kislak Collection

▲ **A Taíno stool**

Do You Speak Arawak?

These words come from the Taíno's language:

hurricane   barbecue   hammock   canoe

The End of a World

Some Taíno communities had populations in the thousands. Then Columbus and the early Spanish explorers arrived.

The Taíno were Arawak-speaking Indians. The Carib, another language group, were their enemies. But the Europeans killed Taíno and Carib alike. The explorers carried diseases that were fatal to the Indians. They took the Indians' land and possessions. Those who didn't die of disease were enslaved or killed.

Within 50 years, the millions of Indians in the Caribbean islands were reduced to a few hundred. The death of so many Taíno and other Indians meant the Spanish needed people to work for them. They brought in African slaves. Other European powers moved into the Caribbean. They did the same.

Sugar and the Slave Trade

In the Caribbean islands Europeans grew nonnative crops like coffee and bananas. African slaves who took the place of Indian slaves did the work.

Then the Dutch started growing sugarcane. Sugar was a luxury in Europe, so it was a very valuable crop. The British established sugar plantations on Jamaica, Barbados, and other smaller islands. These plantations became the British Empire's most valuable possessions. —*Susan Moger*

▼ **A sugar plantation in Haiti, 18th century**

The Taíno Today

Thousands of Taíno descendants are alive and well, in Cuba, the Dominican Republic, Haiti, and the United States. They even live in Spain.

Taíno Indians reunite annually at a conference in Cuba. Said one, "Now we know we are not the last of our kind and are not alone."

Sequence Writing Frame

Use the Writing Frame below to orally summarize "Exploring the United States."

In the 1500's Spanish explorers headed into frontier land that would later become the United States.

In 1528 Cabeza de Vaca was sailing west along the Gulf Coast, when

_____ .

For the next four years _____

_____ .

In 1536 Cabeza de Vaca's group made it to _____

_____ .

In 1538, in search of riches _____ .

They traveled _____ .

Then, in 1542 _____

_____ .

Hernando de Soto never found the treasure he was seeking.

Use the frame to write the summary on another sheet of paper. Be sure to include the **bold** signal words. Keep this as a model of this Text Structure.

Critical Thinking

1 The routes between Africa, the West Indies, and colonial New England are called _____ .

   A. the Middle Passage

   B. the Northwest Passage

   C. triangular trade

2 Point to the place in "Exploring the United States" that describes what *frontier* means.

3 Locate the paragraph in "The Taíno World: Contact and Impact" that explains what the British Empire's most valuable possession was.

4 Review the map "Routes of Spanish Explores, 1513-1603" on page 108. Is Cuba close to New Spain? Share your ideas with a partner.

A scale shows the relationship between distances on a map and real distances.

Digital Learning

For a list of links and activities that relate to this History/Social Science standard, visit the California Treasures Web site at www.macmillanmh.com to access the Content Readers resources. Have children visit the Field Trip "St. Augustine, Florida."

THE FRENCH AND INDIAN WAR

In the 1700s England was not the only European power in North America. France and Spain both claimed lands that were the homelands of Native Americans.

Spain controlled much of what is now the West and Southwest. France claimed most of America's interior. Disagreements between France and England grew when English farmers from Virginia began to settle land claimed by both the French and the English. The conflict is called the **French and Indian War** because the English were fighting the French and their Native American friends, the Wyandot. In 1707, England became Great Britain. Its citizens, now known as British, fought several wars with France that spread to North America.

For the first half of the 1700s, Native Americans were able to keep the French and British colonist out of the Ohio River Valley. Then conflicts among groups there led some to sell their land to the colonist. The colonist wanted to farm the land, but France feared that the British would take over the region and built forts there. The British saw the forts as a threat and decided to drive the French out.

The lieutenant governor of Virginia, Robert Dinwiddie, sent a young George Washington to lead troops to Fort Duquesne (doo•KAIN), located at present-day Pittsburgh. On May 28, 1754, Washington's troops attacked and defeated a small force of French soldiers near the fort.

On July 3, 1754, French soldiers and Indians fired at the British from the woods. Outnumbered, Washington surrendered a day later. His men were allowed to return to Virginia.

France's early victories were made possible with the help of their longtime friends, the Wyandot, whom the French called the Huron, and other Native American groups. Native Americans taught the French how to make surprise attacks on the British from behind trees and large rocks. In contrast, the British marched in the open battlefield in long rows. This made them easy targets.

News of the French victories caused the American colonist to panic. They feared the French would kill them or force them out of North America. The colonist begged British leader William Pitt to provide more help. He began to pour more money, troops, and equipment into the war. This was to be a turning point.

British soldiers passing over the Allegheny Mountains in the French and Indian War

By 1759 the British had won several victories against the French. Greatly encouraged, the British fought even harder. In June numerous British forces attacked Quebec. After three months of fighting, the French surrendered Quebec on September 13. A year later, British general Amherst seized Montreal. This gave Britain control of Canada.

France tried to recover Quebec in 1762, but failed. Meanwhile, in Europe, Great Britain and France continued to fight. Spain aided the French, and in return France agreed to give Spain much of the Louisiana Territory. In 1763, France admitted defeat by Great Britain. Both countries signed the **Treaty of Paris**, which ended the French and Indian War. Britain now had control of former French lands east of the Mississippi River.

In October 1763, news of the Treaty of Paris arrived in North America. The defeated French could no longer help the Native Americans. Nevertheless, Great Britain wanted to keep down the cost of defending North America. To stop British settlements in the Ohio River Valley, Great Britain issued the **Proclamation of 1763**. This proclamation, or official announcement, set aside all British land west of the Appalachians for Native Americans. The proclamation calmed the Indians, but angered colonist who wanted to move there.

As a result of the French and Indian War, American colonists changed the way

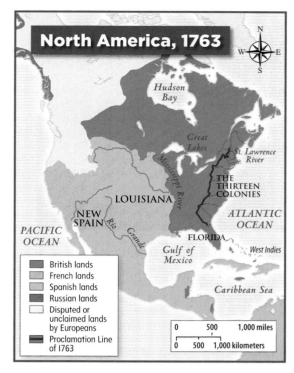

they saw themselves and their county of origin. The colonist had fought against an enemy and won. They proved that they had strong leaders and that they could unite in a common effort. This gave them a feeling of strength.

Angry with Great Britain for the Proclamation of 1763, many colonists continued to move onto the lands west of the Appalachians. Colonist also realized that they could not count on Great Britain to protect them from the Native Americans.

The French and Indian War caused the colonist to unite against Great Britain. Soon they would fight for their own independence.

The French and Indian War

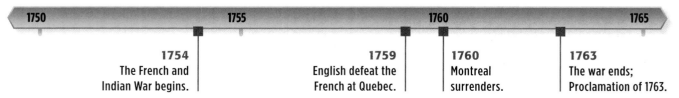

1750 1755 1760 1765

1754
The French and Indian War begins.

1759
English defeat the French at Quebec.

1760
Montreal surrenders.

1763
The war ends; Proclamation of 1763.

The Bridgeman Art Library

English ships arrive in Jamestown.

Jamestown:
Competition, Conflict, and Cooperation
The first English colony in the Americas had a difficult start.

A Business Proposition

Settling Jamestown—the first English colony in what is now the United States—was a business proposition. The 104 English settlers who arrived in 1607 had a mission. They were supposed to cash in on America's treasures for England.

The London Company paid for the trip and expected a return on its investment. But the colonists had picked a terrible spot to settle. The land at Jamestown was swampy, and the settlers were not farmers. They had a choice: trade with the Indians or take food from them by force.

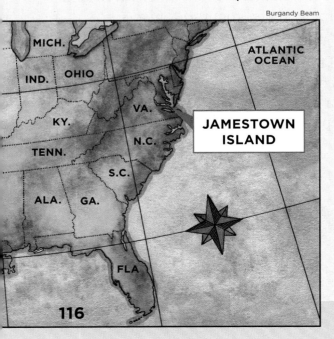

Burgandy Beam

MICH.
IND. OHIO
KY.
TENN.
ALA. GA.
VA.
N.C.
S.C.
FLA
ATLANTIC OCEAN
JAMESTOWN ISLAND

Trade or No Trade

The Indians were the Powhatan. Relations between Indians and settlers were iffy. The settlers built a fort to protect themselves from the Powhatan. They also reached out to them in trade.

Wahunsonacock was chief of the Powhatan. He ruled an empire of 30 tribes and 15,000 people.

The Indians refused to trade for food during the winter of 1609–1610. As a result, most of the colonists starved. In October there were 500 people at Jamestown. The following May, only 60 were left alive.

Relations with Indians: War

As the colonists settled in, the Powhatan became alarmed. Trading posts were one thing. Permanent farms were something else. In 1622 the new leader of the Powhatan raided other settlements along the James River. The Indians killed 347 colonists. That was one-fourth of the total population. Jamestown escaped harm, warned by an Indian boy.

The colonist survivors fought back in July 1624. In a two-day battle, 800 Indian warriors fought 60 well-armed colonists. The Indians lost.

From Tobacco...

The Jamestown colonists found "gold" in tobacco. It was grown on privately owned farms. Indentured servants and African slaves did the work. Indentured servants had to work for seven years. Then they were free. Slaves had to work a lifetime. By the 1670s slaves outnumbered indentured servants in Virginia.

...to Representative Government

In 1618 the first general assembly of burgesses (representatives) was elected. Members were elected by property owners. The assembly's job was to advise the governor. From this seed grew Virginia's

Association for the Preservation of Virginia Antiquities

▲ **A model of the Jamestown settlement**

House of Burgesses. That's where George Washington and Thomas Jefferson got their start.

America's Birthplace

Jamestown left a record of greed, war, and death. It also left a legacy of bravery, resilience, cultural diversity, and the beginning of representative government. —*Adapted from TIME*

John Smith Visits the Chief

John Smith was a leader of Jamestown colony. He described his visit to Wahunsonacock in December 1607:
"He sat covered with a great robe, made of raccoon skins, and all the tails hanging by. . ."
Around him were "two rows of men and behind them as many women, with all their heads and shoulders painted red."

Stock Montage/Getty Images

TIME FOR KIDS

117

Problem/Solution Writing Frame

Use the Writing Frame below to orally summarize "Jamestown: Competition, Conflict, and Cooperation."

The first English colony in the Americas had a difficult start.

This **problem occurred** because _____

_____ .

One solution was to _____ .

The settlers felt in danger **because** _____ .

To solve this _____ .

The Powhatan became alarmed because _____

_____ .

The result was _____ .

Jamestown escaped **because** _____ .

In the two-day battle, 800 Indian warriors fought 60 well-armed

colonists. **The result was** _____

_____ .

Use the frame to write the summary on another sheet of paper. Be sure to include the **bold** signal words. Keep this as a model of this Text Structure.

Critical Thinking

1 The French and Indian War was a conflict
between _____ .

    A. English and French

    B. French and Indian

    C. Indian and English

2 Find the meaning of *indentured servant* in
"Jamestown: Competition, Conflict, and Cooperation."

3 Was the Proclamation of 1763 a success? Locate
the paragraph in "The French and Indian War"
that helps you form an answer.

4 Review the time line on page 115. Talk to a partner
about the length of the French and Indian War.

A time line highlights
key events that
happened during a
certain time period.

Digital Learning

For a list of links and activities that relate to this History/Social
Science standard, visit the California Treasures Web site at
www.macmillanmh.com to access the Content Readers resources.
Have children view the video "The Struggle for North America."

CONFLICTS IN THE COLONY

Conflicts existed between the English colonists and their Native American neighbors in almost every colony. Most of the conflicts happened when colonist settled lands that native peoples thought of as their own.

In Virginia the **Powhatan Wars** were a series of conflicts that went on for nearly 40 years. Chief Powhatan had helped the first colonist in Jamestown. During the "starving time" in 1610, the Powhatans had taken pity on the hungry colonists and let them stay in Powhatan villages.

A new governor, Lord de la Warr, arrived in Virginia in 1610. He thought the colonists had been kidnapped, and he ordered Powhatan to return them. Powhatan refused to be ordered around. Their disagreement soon led to fighting.

The colonists destroyed Powhatan crops and stole their food, but an even worse enemy attacked the Native Americans. Diseases brought by the colonists killed thousands of them. As many as 90 percent of the Powhatan may have died from diseases such as measles.

While they were dying, more colonists were arriving from England. There were 18,000 English settlers in Virginia by 1650. Gradually the number of Indians declined until they were unable to resist colonial settlements.

In 1636 war broke out between the Pequot and the colonists at Plymouth. **The Pequot War** began because the Pequot feared that their lands would be taken by the new colonist spreading across New England.

The English planned a brutal, surprise attack. They surrounded a wooden Pequot fort and set fire to it. The Pequot were killed or captured as they ran from their homes.

There were few survivors. Those who did escape the attack were captured and sold into slavery. By 1638 the Pequot were reduced to a few dozen people. They signed their lands over to the English and went to live with other nearby Native Americans.

The defeat of the Pequot weakened the power of Native Americans in New England and opened up new territory for English colonists. Soon English settlers were moving into areas which are now part of New Hampshire, Vermont, and Maine.

English settlers attacked the Pequot village at Missituck (now Mystic), Connecticut, in the spring of 1637. ▶

▲ **Wampanoag Indians attack a farm during King Philip's War.**

King Philip's War began in 1675 and lasted for more than a year. It was a brutal war, and terrible attacks took place on both sides. It started when Metacomet became leader of the Wampanoag. The English colonial governor called Metacomet Philip and Metacomet became known as King Philip to the English colonists. He was determined to stop the English from taking any more land. He sent messengers to his longtime enemies, the Narragansett, asking for their help. They refused, but other Native American groups decided to join Metacomet.

In August 1676, Native American scouts helped the colonists track down Metacomet in the swamp where he was hiding. The Wampanoag leader was killed by a Native American ally of the colonist.

With Metacomet's death, King Philip's War ended. About 4,000 Native Americans had been killed, and most of the remaining Wampanoag, including Metacomet's wife and son, were sold into slavery in the West Indies. Native American power in New England was over.

The Yamasee were originally allies of the Carolina colonist, but in 1715 the **Yamasee War** began.

The Yamasee complained that the English did not pay them for rescuing **hostages**, or prisoners, from other Native Americans. They had also built up large debts to English traders. The Yamasee were afraid they would be enslaved to settle their debts.

The Yamasee got weapons from Spanish colonist in Florida. They attacked the colonist in 1715. The Yamasee had a much larger army, and it looked as if their enemies would lose. Then the colonist got help from the Cherokee in January 1716.

In 1717 the Yamasee were defeated and fled to Florida. The Cherokee then became the most powerful Native Americans in the Carolinas.

The Trail of Tears

Defying the United States Supreme Court, President Andrew Jackson forced thousands of Cherokee people to leave their land.

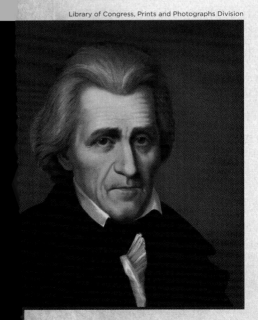

▲ **European settlers meet with Indians in what is now Georgia.**

▲ **Andrew Jackson**

From the time that Europeans settled in North America, they were in conflict with the people who were already there, called American Indians. There were and are many different Indian Nations across the continent.

The Indian Removal Act

In 1828 the people of the Cherokee Nation lived in north Georgia. Their land was rich in gold. Members of the U. S. government wanted control of that wealth.

In 1830 Congress passed the Indian Removal Act. President Andrew Jackson signed the act, which would force the Cherokee off their land. Senators Daniel Webster and Davy Crockett fought for the Cherokee's rights.

Even the U. S. Supreme Court disagreed with President Jackson. The justices said that the Cherokee Nation was sovereign, meaning that it was a country. That meant that the U.S. Congress could not control the use of Cherokee land. The Cherokee would have to agree to their removal in a treaty. The treaty would then have to be ratified by the U.S. Senate.

In 1835 two members of the Cherokee tribe, Major Ridge and Elias Boudinot, signed a treaty that would remove the Cherokee from their land. Most of the Cherokee people disagreed, but the Senate ratified the treaty. It passed by just one vote.

A painting of the Trail of Tears

TIME FOR KIDS

Nunna daul Tsuny

In 1838 the United States started moving the Cherokee people to Oklahoma. General John Wood, who was ordered to move the tribe, refused. He resigned in protest. But a replacement, General Winfield Scott, soon returned with 7,000 soldiers.

The U.S. Army forced 17,000 men, women, and children from their land. The Cherokees were herded into shelters and then forced to march 1,000 miles. They were short on food, blankets, and medicine. More than 4,000 people died along the way.

The route they traveled and the journey itself became known as the Trail of Tears. In Cherokee the name is Nunna daul Tsuny, meaning the trail where they cried.

Cherokee traditions are still alive. ▶

What Happened Next

Senator Davy Crockett lost his seat in Congress because he supported the Cherokee people. The Cherokee killed Major Ridge, his son, and Elias Boudinot.

The Cherokee land was available to gold prospectors. Soon they were everywhere. In 1849, when gold was discovered in California, the prospectors moved on, leaving ghost towns behind.

The Cherokee people, however, continued their traditions in Oklahoma. Today the people of the Cherokee Nation run schools, health programs, casinos, and more. They also keep alive the memory of those who suffered and died on the Trail of Tears.

Sequence Writing Frame

Use the Writing Frame below to orally summarize "The Trail of Tears."

From the time that Europeans settled North America, they were in conflict with the people who were already there. One of these people was the Cherokee Nation in north Georgia.

In 1828 _____ .

Not long after that, in 1830, _____

_____ .

At the same time, the U.S. Supreme Court _____

_____ .

The justices said _____ .

Then, in 1835, _____ .

By 1838 _____ .

The route they traveled became known as _____

_____ .

Today, the Cherokee Nation is active in Oklahoma.

Use the frame to write the summary on another sheet of paper. Be sure to include the **bold** signal words. Keep this as a model of this Text Structure.

Critical Thinking

1. The 1636 war between Native Americans and the colonists at Plymouth is _____.

   A. the Powhatan War

   B. the Pequot War

   C. King Philip's War

2. Point to the word in "Conflicts in the Colony" that is similar to *prisoner*.

3. Reread the paragraph in "Trail of Tears" that explains the term sovereign nation.

4. Orally create your own caption for the painting of Andrew Jackson on page 122.

Captions give the reader additional information about the subject of the article.

Digital Learning

For a list of links and activities that relate to this History/ Social Science standard, visit the California Treasures Web site at www.macmillanmh.com to access the Content Readers resources. Have children view the video "The English Establish 13 Colonies."

WILLIAM PENN FOUNDS A COLONY

In 1651 King Charles II fled from a **revolution** in England. A revolution is a change of government. Admiral William Penn, a friend of the king, loaned the king money and helped him return to England in 1660. King Charles never forgot his friend's loyalty.

The admiral's son, also named William Penn, inherited a large fortune when his father died in 1670. King Charles did not repay his loan. However, more than money, Penn wanted land for a colony.

Penn belonged to the Society of Friends. Members of the Society were jailed and even killed for their beliefs. Penn himself had been jailed several times.

He decided that in his colony, he would allow tolerance for all religions.

In 1681, King Charles gave Penn land in North America and asked him to name his colony Pennsylvania (Penn's woods) to honor Penn's father and the king's friend.

William Penn wanted a place where all Christians could worship without fear. He called his colony a **Holy Experiment** to prove that people of different beliefs could live together peacefully.

In 1682 Penn wrote *The Frame of the Government of Pennsylvania*. Penn included in his government plan freedom of worship and the right to a trial by jury.

▼ **Many of the German settlers of Pennsylvania were hard-working and successful farmers.**

William Penn advertised in England and in Europe for new colonists. The promise of religious freedom, cheap land, and booming trade brought thousands of colonists to Pennsylvania.

One German wrote about his voyage to Pennsylvania in 1683: "My company consisted of many sorts of people. . . They were not only different in respect to their occupations, but were also of such different religions and behaviors that I might . . . compare the ship . . . with Noah's Ark."

Many Germans came to Pennsylvania because wars had caused great destruction and hunger. Some of the German immigrants belonged to a religious group called the Mennonites. They were often called the plain people because they dressed simply.

Descendants of German settlers in Pennsylvania are called Pennsylvania Dutch. These settlers were German not Dutch, but the word *Deutsch* (DOYch), means "German" in the German language.

In spite of the long, often dangerous voyage across the Atlantic Ocean, immigrants continued to flood into the colony. "Poor People . . . ", one colonist wrote, "get three times the Wages for their Labor then they can in England."

In addition to settlers from Germany, England, and Wales, Pennsylvania attracted many Scots-Irish. The Scots-Irish were people from Scotland who settled in Ireland in the early 1600s. They left Ireland because they did not find freedom or prosperity there. Many of these independent-minded colonists settled in the Pennsylvania backcountry, which was land on the fringes of colonial settlement.

William Penn wanted his colony to have a port on the Atlantic Ocean. Part of the New York colony that bordered Pennsylvania had an Atlantic coastline. Penn asked the Duke of York, the brother of King Charles II and another of Penn's friends, to give him an area of southern New York colony called the Three Lower Counties. Today this area is the state of Delaware.

The Duke sold the land to Penn. However, the colonists of the Three Lower Counties were Dutch, Swedish, and Finnish, and they wanted to make laws for themselves. In 1702 Penn allowed this area to have its own lawmaking assembly. However, Pennsylvania's governor ruled Delaware until 1776, when the American Revolution began.

Religion in the American Colonies

Religion played an important part in the lives of early English settlers in the American colonies.

▲ Colonists on their way to church

Bettmann/Corbis

People who settled in the English colonies in America came from places where religion was controlled by the government. Some came here to get away from one religion and set up another. Some came to find religious freedom and offer it to others.

The Puritans—Massachusetts

The goal of the Puritans was to separate themselves from the Church of England and to purify it. They were persecuted in England for their beliefs. In America they practiced their religion and excluded all others. The Massachusetts Bay Colony was governed by Puritans. They did not tolerate other beliefs. They did not consider women equal to men in any way. They expelled those who disagreed with them.

At a Glance: Religion in Five American Colonies

Colony	Founded By	Religion	Tolerant of Other Religions?
Virginia	Virginia Company	Church of England	No
Massachusetts	Separatists	Purified Church of England	No
Rhode Island	Roger Williams	Any	Yes
Maryland	Calvert Family	Catholic; Church of England	Of all Christians
Pennsylvania	William Penn	Any	Yes

The Quakers—Pennsylvania

Quakers' beliefs were different from the Puritans'. Quakers believed the Holy Spirit was in every person and ministers and priests were not necessary. They did not believe that governments should impose religion on their citizens. They considered women the equal of men. These ideas got them in trouble with the Puritans in Massachusetts.

William Penn, an English Quaker, established a colony called Pennsylvania. In Pennsylvania, all religions were respected.

Catholic Church—Maryland

In Europe, Catholics and Protestants were deadly enemies. The Calvert family, who founded Maryland, were Catholic. Unlike many other people of their time, they believed Catholics and Protestants could live together peacefully. In 1649, Maryland extended freedom of religion to other Christians.

Church of England—Virginia

The Church of England was the official religion of England. In Virginia, it was the only religion allowed. Virginia's House of Burgesses enacted harsh religious laws. Virginia colonists were required to convert Native Americans to Christianity. The most famous convert in Virginia was Pocahontas. —*Lisa Jo Rudy*

The Granger Collection

▲ **A Quaker meeting in Philadelphia**

Jews in Rhode Island

In 1638, Roger Williams was expelled from the Massachusetts colony for his beliefs. A Puritan minister, he had split with the colony's leaders. He founded Rhode Island, a colony open to all religions. In 1658, Jews arrived in Newport, Rhode Island, seeking religious liberty. There, Touro Synagogue was built. It was the first permanent Jewish house of worship in America.

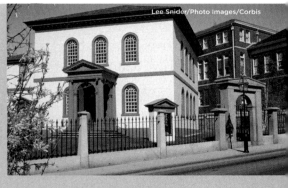
Lee Snider/Photo Images/Corbis

▲ Touro Synagogue today

Problem/Solution Writing Frame

Use the Writing Frame below to orally summarize "William Penn Founds a Colony."

In England, members of the Society of Friends were jailed and even killed

for their beliefs. **To help solve this problem**, William Penn _____

_____

_____

_____ .

Penn needed land in North America for his new colony. **To solve this**

problem, King Charles _____

_____

_____ .

The result was _____

_____

_____ .

Use the frame to write the summary on another sheet of paper.
Be sure to include the **bold** signal words. Keep this as a model of
this Text Structure.

Critical Thinking

1. The Holy Experiment colony would later become _____.

   A. Delaware

   B. Pennsylvania

   C. New York

2. Find the meaning of *revolution* in "William Penn Founds a Colony."

3. Locate the paragraph in "Religion in the American Colonies" that explains what the Quakers believed.

4. Review the chart on page 128. Discuss with a partner which colony you would have gone to and why.

Charts may show different categories to help the reader organize information.

Digital Learning

For a list of links and activities that relate to this History/Social Science standard, visit the California Treasures Web site at www.macmillanmh.com to access the Content Readers resources. Have children view the Biography "Anne Hutchinson."

SELF-GOVERNMENT

The Virginia House of Burgesses was founded in 1619, and was the oldest elected **assembly** in the Americas. An assembly is a lawmaking body. Some assemblies had more power than others, however.

Colonial assemblies gathered to make laws. This **legislation** was an important step on the road to self-government. Legislation is the making or passing of laws. However, every law had to be approved by a governor or by the government in London.

Colonial self-government did not apply to everyone. The first voters had to be white males who owned land. Later a small number of men who did not own land could vote and be elected to assemblies. Women, indentured servants, enslaved Africans, and Native Americans could not vote or hold office.

There were differences among the colonial assemblies, but they also shared some common powers. First of all, each assembly passed laws and controlled how its colony's money would be spent. This meant they also controlled the salaries of colonial officials.

Second, assemblies were guaranteed in each colony's charter, so colonist knew they had a right to express their opinions through the assemblies.

Finally, since members of assemblies were elected, they were popular with the colonists and represented their views.

The colonial assemblies used the English lawmaking body, called Parliament, as their model. Colonists saw themselves as free English citizens. The Virginia Charter stated this when it said that Virginia's colonists would have the same freedoms "as if they had been . . . born" in England.

Assemblies formed the elected part of colonial government. Colonial governors were usually appointed either by the king or by the proprietor, or owner of the colony. By 1750 there were eight royal governors and three proprietary governors. Connecticut and Rhode Island elected their own governors.

This illustration of a town meeting shows that only wealthy white men took part. ▶

Most colonial governors were chosen to represent the interest of the king or the proprietor. Therefore, they were not usually popular with the colonists.

The governor could reject any law passed by a colonial assembly. Then the assembly might appeal to the English government in London for support, and the governor would have to explain his objection to the king or proprietor.

The governors of some colonies had the power to close the assembly. Governors and assemblies had to cooperate because the assembly controlled the money the governor needed to run the colony.

The assembly dealt with business that concerned the entire colony. The colonies also had officials who made decisions about the government responsibilities of towns and counties.

Justices, or judges, supervised colonial courts. The governor and the assembly selected colonists to serve as judges. Local courts settled disputes between individuals or answered questions about the law.

Each county had a sheriff. A lawbreaker might have to spend time in the public **pillory**. A pillory is a wooden frame with holes for a person's neck and hands. The public embarrassment was considered a punishment for minor offenses such as swearing. More serious crimes, such as robbery, could be punished by whipping or even death.

Colonial elections were much different from modern elections. First of all, candidates spoke to colonists one at a time. On Election Day, voting was usually public. Voters in some colonies had to sign their names on paper ballots to prevent them from voting twice.

"Treating" was another Election Day difference. Candidates were expected to buy food and drinks for voters.

A slave pen like the one recreated at the museum

Honoring Freedom

This museum preserves the story of a historic quest for freedom.

The National Underground Railroad Freedom Center honors those who fought for freedom through the Underground Railroad. The Underground Railroad was a network of people who made it possible for those held in slavery to find freedom. The museum is in Cincinnati, Ohio, just across the Ohio River from Kentucky, a former slave state.

Slavery in the United States

Slavery began in the United States in the 1600s and went on for more than 200 years. In that time millions of people were kidnapped from their homes in Africa and brought to North America as slaves. Even after the slave trade with Africa ended, slavery continued.

The first African slaves came ashore at Jamestown, Virginia, in the 1600s. Over the course of two centuries, slavery took a

firm hold in the colonies and remained a part of the new nation. Enslaved people had no rights. Their children were not thought of as their own. Families were torn apart when slaves were sold. Slaves were often abused. They were not permitted an education.

The one bright spot in this terrible history is the story of brave men and women who resisted it. Thousands risked their lives to help enslaved people find freedom. More slaves than we can ever know escaped or resisted their masters.

Bettmann/Corbis

A slave market

Former Slaves Speak

In the 1930s many people who had once been slaves were still living. More than 2,300 of them were interviewed through the Federal Writers' Project, part of the Works Progress Administration.

These selections are from their stories.

Marilda Pethy, no age given

"Why, I've seen people handcuffed together and driven . . . like cattle . . . I had two brothers and two sisters sold, and we never did see them [again]. . . . When I was nine or ten years old I was put up on the block to be sold . . . They were offered $600, but my mistress cried so much that master did not sell me."

Sarah Frances Shaw Graves, age 87

"I was born March 23, 1850, in Kentucky, somewhere near Louisville. I was brought to Missouri when I was six months old, along with my mama . . .We left my papa in Kentucky. . . My papa never knew where my mama went, and my mama never knew where papa went."

John W. Fields, age 89

"We took advantage of every opportunity to educate ourselves . . . [But] plantation owners were very harsh if we were caught trying to learn or write."

Cruel Reminder— The Slave Pen

One exhibit is called the slave pen. It is the actual wooden structure used by Captain John Anderson, a slave dealer, to lock up his slaves. Visitors can enter the slave pen's cramped space. They can imagine being locked in it with dozens of other enslaved people waiting to be sold.

Slave pens were common sights throughout the upper South, a region important in the interstate slave trade. The exhibit is a chilling reminder of slavery.

Make a Difference

At the Freedom Center, visitors can walk through the Hall of Everyday Heroes and learn about people who helped others find freedom. Naomi Nelson is the center's director of education. She hopes that the museum shows people that they can stand up and make a difference. —*Susan Moger*

135

Description Writing Frame

Use the Writing Frame below to orally summarize "Honoring Freedom."

The history of slavery in the United States is a sad and terrible one.

For example, enslaved people _____

_____ .

Families were _____

_____ .

Besides that, slaves were not permitted _____

_____ .

Slaves were often abused. **For example**, many slave owners in the

upper South had slave pens. **They were used** _____

_____ .

Because of these things, thousands _____

_____ .

Use the frame to write the summary on another sheet of paper.
Be sure to include the **bold** signal words. Keep this as a model of
this Text Structure.

Critical Thinking

1. A lawmaking body is called _____.

   A. legislation

   B. assembly

   C. Parliament

2. Point to the sentence in "Self-Government" that describes the first voters.

3. Reread the paragraph in "Self-Government" that explains how lawbreakers were dealt with in the colonies.

4. Orally create your own caption for the photo of the slave pen on page 134.

> Captions give the reader additional information about the subject of the article.

Digital Learning

For a list of links and activities that relate to this History/Social Science standard, visit the California Treasures Web site at www.macmillanmh.com to access the Content Readers resources. Have children view A Day in the Life "Enslaved Young People in the Colonies During the 1700s."

137

PROTESTING NEW TAXES

The French-Indian War ended in 1763. The victory had cost the British government a huge amount of money. The government felt that it had spent much of this money to protect the colonists in America. George III and his advisers decided to tax the American colonies to pay for some of the debt.

In 1764 the British government passed the **Sugar Act**, which forced the colonists to pay a tax on all sugar products. Colonists who ignored the new Sugar Act were arrested and fined.

In 1765 the British government passed the **Stamp Act**. Every letter, newspaper, pamphlet, and legal document—every printed item—had to have an official stamp. Colonists paid for the stamps.

The colonists did not like these taxes. More important, though, was that the money went to Great Britain, not to the colonial government. Colonists began to complain that they had to pay taxes they had not voted for.

A few months later the British government passed the **Quartering Act**. It allowed British officials to put soldiers into colonists' homes. The Quartering Act was only for the colonies. The colonists began to feel that the British government was treating them unfairly.

Every colony protested the new law. In October 1765, representatives from nine colonies met in New York City at what is called the Stamp Act Congress.

This congress announced that Parliament—the British legislature—had no right to tax the colonists because they could not vote in elections for the members of Parliament. This was against British legal traditions.

The Stamp Act went into effect on November 1. That day, almost all colonists boycotted the stamps. To **boycott** means to refuse to do business with, or buy goods from, a person, group, or country.

Men and women gave up tea and other British goods. The boycott soon began to hurt British merchants. In 1766, because of the boycott, Parliament voted to **repeal**, or end, the Stamp Act.

In 1767 Parliament passed the **Townshend Acts**, named for Charles Townshend, the treasurer of the British government. Taxes were to be paid on manufactured goods—such as paper, glass, lead, and paint—imported from Great Britain.

The colonists knew they were strong when they acted together. They agreed to boycott the new taxed items and anyone who continued to sell or use taxed goods.

The British government repealed the Townshend Acts, but it passed the Tea Act in March of 1773. **The Tea Act** said that the British East India Company did not have to charge tax on its tea, but that American tea merchants did. The act angered American merchants because it made their tea more expensive.

Patriots, disguised as Mohawk Indians, threw British tea into Boston Harbor.

In late November 1773, three British East India Company ships entered Boston Harbor. People in Boston refused to allow the ship to unload. The governor of Massachusetts, Thomas Hutchinson, ordered the ships to stay in the harbor until the tea was sold.

On the night of December 16, 1773, about 50 Sons of Liberty, some disguised as Mohawk Indians, boarded the ships. They broke open the tea chests and emptied them into the harbor. This attack became known as the Boston Tea Party.

An angry Parliament punished the colonists of Boston. Boston Harbor was closed until the colonists paid for the tea. Town meetings were banned. Colonists called Parliament's actions the Intolerable Acts. Intolerable means "unbearable." The Intolerable Acts united the colonies against Great Britain. Representatives of the colonies met in Philadelphia to discuss the problem at what became known as the First Continental Congress.

The First Continental Congress met in September 1774. Representatives discussed how to fight the Intolerable Acts. They sent King George III a **petition**, or written request, signed by many people. In their petition, the representatives asked the king to repeal the acts they found intolerable.

At the same time the representatives agreed to boycott trade with Great Britain again. Some representatives feared that there might be fighting, so each colony was asked to organize groups of **minutemen**. Minutemen were young men who would assemble at a minute's notice to defend their towns.

Samuel Adams realized that the colonies had to be able to contact each other quickly. The only way to do this was by writing letters. By 1774 Correspondence Committees were formed in all of the colonies. People throughout the colonies could share their ideas and worries. Difficult choices faced the colonists as they decided what to do next.

HOW THEY CHOSE THESE WORDS FOR THE
Declaration of Independence

The writing of the Declaration of Independence was assigned to Thomas Jefferson, but he had some help.

In 1776 the Continental Congress prepared to vote on the question of American independence. But before it could vote, Congress needed a written declaration to explain the decision.

Congress established a committee to draft the Declaration of Independence. It included Benjamin Franklin, John Adams, Connecticut merchant Roger Sherman, and New York lawyer Robert Livingston. Thomas Jefferson was the chairman of the committee. It was his job to write the first draft of the declaration.

Jefferson was only 33 and was not the most important person on the committee. So why was he the writer? Other members of the committee were involved in other work that they felt was more important. Benjamin Franklin was sick in bed.

So Jefferson sat down to write the Declaration of Independence. He wrote in a home on Market Street in Philadelphia. He started with the words "When in the course of human events . . ."

His writing went on to attack the King of England. In those days, attacking the King in writing meant you were declaring a revolution.

Benjamin Franklin, John Adams, and Thomas Jefferson working on the Declaration of Independence ▶

Bettmann/Corbis

▲ **Thomas Jefferson**

Jefferson used his own poetic style of writing. He drew a lot of his ideas and words, though, from other writers. He sounded a bit like Benjamin Franklin. He sounded a little like the philosopher John Locke. He actually copied from the Declaration of Rights that George Mason had written for the Constitution of Virginia. In those days, copying was considered to be proper and showed that you had read a great deal.

Once he finished his draft, Jefferson showed it to Franklin. Franklin made some changes. Among other things, he changed the phrase "We hold these truths to be sacred and undeniable" to the now-famous words "We hold these truths to be self-evident."

On July 2, 1776, the Continental Congress read Jefferson's Declaration. They made a great many changes, and Jefferson was quite upset. Finally, though, the entire Congress agreed on a single document.

At the official signing of the parchment copy on August 2, John Hancock, the president of the Congress, penned his name with his famous flourish. "There must be no pulling different ways," he declared. "We must all hang together." According to the early American historian Jared Sparks, Franklin replied, "Yes, we must, indeed, all hang together, or most assuredly we shall all hang separately." —*Lisa Jo Rudy*

▼ **The signed Declaration of Independence**

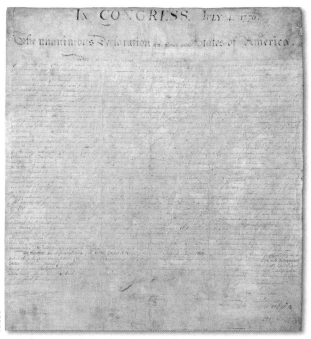

NARA

141

Cause/Effect Writing Frame

Use the Writing Frame below to orally summarize "Protesting New Taxes."

There were several **causes** for the colonist's boycott of the taxed goods.

One **cause** was the passing of the Sugar Act. The **effect** was

colonists_____.

Colonists who did not pay the tax _____.

Another cause for the boycott was the passing of the Quartering

Act. Only people in the colonies had to _____

_____.

This explains why _____.

In addition, the Tea Act said that _____

_____.

This **caused** American merchants _____

_____.

For all of these reasons the colonists agreed to boycott.

Use the frame to write the summary on another sheet of paper. Be sure to include the **bold** signal words. Keep this as a model of this Text Structure.

Critical Thinking

1. The _____ Act taxed manufactured goods imported from Great Britain.

    A. Tea

    B. Townshend

    C. Quartering

2. Point to the sentence in "Protesting New Taxes" that provides a definition of the word *repeal*.

3. Locate the paragraph in "How They Chose These Words for the Declaration of Independence" that explains why people did not attack the king in writing.

4. Review the painting of the writing of the Declaration of Independence on page 140. Discuss with a partner how this picture supports the text.

Photographs and captions give visual examples that help explain what the text states.

Digital Learning

For a list of links and activities that relate to this History/Social Science standard, visit the California Treasures Web site at www.macmillanmh.com to access the Content Readers resources. Have children view the video "The Struggle for North America."

AMERICANS OF THE REVOLUTION

The **American Revolution** was the war between Great Britain and its 13 colonies. From 1775–1783 many great Americans help shape the ideas that led to the founding of the United States of America. Here are the biographies of two of these Americans.

Abigail Adams 1744–1818

Girls in colonial America did not always go to school. New England had some schools, and Abigail Smith had a father who encouraged all of his children, his daughters as well as his son, to read anything they liked. As she grew up, Smith continued to read about a wide variety of subjects.

In 1764 Smith married John Adams. In 1797 John Adams became the Second President of the United States. Because her husband was often away from home on business, Abigail Adams wrote hundreds of letters to him. Some of her letters give excellent information about events of her time. Other letters offer wise political advice.

Adams opposed slavery. She also strongly believed that women should have the same opportunities and rights as men. This included equal education as well as political rights. She once wrote her husband, "Remember the ladies, and be more generous and favorable to them than your ancestors."

Adams died in 1818, but she is still remembered as one of the first Americans to demand equal rights for women.

The Life of Abigail Adams

1740	1760	1780	1800	1820
1744 Born in Weymouth, Mass.	1764 Marries John Adams	1774 Manages family farm	1800 Moves to the White House	1818 Dies in Quincy, Mass.

The Life of George Washington

1730	1740	1750	1760	1770	1780	1790	1800

1732
Born in Virginia,
February 22

1775
Becomes commander
in chief of the
Continental army

1789
Becomes the first
President of the
United States

1799
Dies on
December 14

George Washington 1732–1799

"I cannot tell a lie!" Young George Washington looked at his angry father and admitted he had used the new ax to cut down his father's cherry tree. But this famous story about George Washington never happened! The story was written to show how honest Washington had always been.

Washington grew up in Westmoreland County, Virginia. When he was about 12 years old, he copied 110 rules for "good behavior" in his notebook. Honesty was important to him even at this early age. He wrote, "be Careful to keep your Promise."

Washington grew into a tall young man of surprising strength and character. Governor Dinwiddie of Virginia put him in command of Virginia's troops during the French and Indian War. Washington learned he could inspire soldiers with his leadership.

In 1775 the Continental Congress elected Washington commander in chief of the Continental army. Although Washington often felt discouraged during the American Revolution, his soldiers trusted and followed him because they knew he was honest and brave. His leadership not only gave his war-tired soldiers hope but also later helped him to become the first President of the United States.

The (Federalist) Party's Over

Being against a "successful" war helped put an end to one of America's first political parties.

In the late 1700s the Federalist Party was in power in the new United States of America. George Washington, Alexander Hamilton, and John Adams were all Federalists, and they had all accomplished great things.

By 1800, though, most people thought the Federalists cared only for themselves. And so the Republicans came into power. The Federalists remained important only in New England.

Then a war began between Britain and France. The first two Republican Presidents, Thomas Jefferson and James Madison, tried to keep the United States out of the struggle. But in 1812, Madison and Congress declared war on Britain. The United States was officially engaged in the War of 1812.

Madison said he really didn't want to go to war at all. He argued that he had been driven to fight by British "outrages" against U.S. shipping. The British navy was stopping American vessels on the high seas and seizing goods and sailors.

Bettmann/Corbis

▲ **George Washington, a Federalist, is sworn in as President of the United States.**

The Federalists were strongly against the war. They felt that the country was not ready for a war. They were worried about losing England as a trading partner. And they were afraid that the United States would lose.

The War of 1812 had glorious successes and humiliating defeats for the United States. American frigates beat British ships. Detroit fell to the enemy. The British tried, and failed, to take Lake Champlain in upstate New York. They burned Washington but were stopped outside Baltimore. Then they prepared to attack New Orleans.

The United States was in real danger. Some of the more radical Federalists wanted to break up the country, separating New England and New York from the rest of the states. More moderate Federalists wanted to use federal tax dollars to defend their states. They also wanted to pass a law keeping their citizens from being drafted into military service for the war.

Before the Federalists could present their proposals to the government, the Americans and the British agreed to a peace treaty.

The war was seen as a success for the Republicans. The Federalists gained a bad reputation as defeatists and traitors. The last Federalist presidential candidate ran in 1816, winning only three states. Federalism became a bad word. Today, the Federalist Party doesn't exist.

▲ **Burning of Washington by the British, 1812**

▲ **The Treaty of Ghent, signed 1814, ended the war and the influence of the Federalists.**

◄ **Battle between American and British ships during the War of 1812**

Francis G. Mayer/Corbis

147

Sequence Writing Frame

Use the Writing Frame below to orally summarize "The (Federalist) Party's Over."

In the late 1700s, the Federalist Party was in power in the new United States of America.

By 1800 _____

_____.

After that _____.

Then a war began _____.

In 1812, Madison and Congress _____.

During the war some Federalist _____

_____.

Then the war was seen _____.

Federalists gained a bad reputation for _____

_____.

Today, _____.

Use the frame to write the summary on another sheet of paper. Be sure to include the **bold** signal words. Keep this as a model of this Text Structure.

Critical Thinking

1. George Washington, Alexander Hamilton, and John Adams were _____.

    A. Federalists

    B. Republicans

    C. Democrats

2. Find the sentence in "Americans of the Revolution" that explains Abigail Adams's views on slavery.

3. Find the paragraph in "The (Federalist) Party's Over" that describes some of the successes and defeats of the War of 1812.

4. Study the time line on page 145. Was George Washington a young man when he became President? Discuss with a partner.

A time line is a quick way to present a lot of information in an organized way.

Digital Learning

For a list of links and activities that relate to this History/Social Science standard, visit the California Treasures Web site at www.macmillanmh.com to access the Content Readers resources. Have children view the Biography "Abigail Adams."

THE WAR BEGINS

What began as a battle of ideas between the British and the colonists turned into a bitter war in 1775. As Joseph Plumb Martin and other American soldiers headed off into battle, little did they know that the fighting would drag on for eight long and deadly years.

Americans who supported the Revolution were called **Patriots**. During the war, Patriot men—mostly young and inexperienced—became soldiers. African American Patriots joined the cause because they hoped that winning the war would put an end to slavery, as the Declaration of Independence promised. Women also helped. Some followed husbands or brothers to the battlefields as cooks or nurses. Others tended farms or shops left behind by men.

Even though they rallied to fight the British, Patriots from the different states were far from united. One of their biggest challenges was to find ways to cooperate to fight Great Britain. After all, it was one of the world's most powerful countries with one of its mightiest armies.

Because the states were now independent, each needed its own government. So each state held a **convention**, a formal meeting, to write a constitution, or plan of government. The new country also needed some form of national government to help it govern the states.

During the war the Second Continental Congress became the national government.

In 1777 it passed the Articles of Confederation, which was the first written plan for an American government. The Articles of Confederation gave most of the governing power to the states, which made the Continental Congress a weak government. The Congress had no legal power to vote for taxes or to force states to send soldiers or supplies for war. With a weak Continental Congress, the British had great advantages at the beginning of the war. The Patriots, however, were fighting for freedom in their own land. This desire for independence led to important American victories.

On Christmas night 1776, George Washington led 2,400 soldiers across the Delaware River. Washington's army reached Trenton, New Jersey, at dawn and attacked the enemy at once. Washington's army forced the Hessians, German soldiers fighting for the British, to surrender. Then traveling quickly on back roads, the Americans attacked the British at Princeton, New Jersey, on January 2, 1777. The British surrendered, and the American army had another victory.

The defeat at New Jersey made the British realize they would not win the war easily. In 1777 they had a new plan. The British decided to capture the Hudson River Valley. This would cut New York and New Jersey off from other states, making it difficult to get supplies. British general John Burgoyne (bur•GOYN) was certain that he could beat the Americans with this plan.

In late summer of 1777, General Burgoyne led his troops south from Canada toward New York. As he traveled, Burgoyne had hoped for help from Iroquois and Mohawk allies. However, Native Americans no longer believed that the British could prevent settlement of their lands. Without Native American scouts to gather information, Burgoyne did not know how many American troops would be waiting for him in New York.

The Americans, on the other hand, knew all about Burgoyne and his forces. Under the leadership of General Horatio Gates, the American army had prepared for a British attack near Saratoga, New York. They had nearly three times as many soldiers as the British. In addition, Gates had sent out groups of Virginia soldiers led by Daniel Morgan to attack the British as they moved toward Saratoga. These soldiers were expert riflemen. They made constant surprise attacks on the British, making the Redcoats weaker as they approached the main American army.

In September 1777, Burgoyne's troops battled American soldiers at Saratoga. By October the British were running out of food. They were also losing men daily to riflemen hidden in the hillsides. After two months of fighting, Burgoyne's discouraged troops were forced to surrender on October 17,1777. Victory at Saratoga ended up changing the direction of the war.

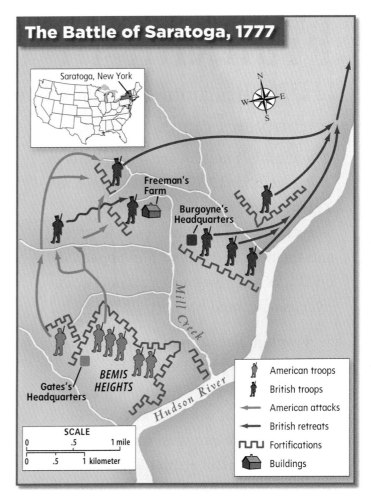

The American victory at Saratoga helped convince Europeans that the young United States might win the war. For years, American leaders had hoped France and other nations would help them fight the British. After the battle of Saratoga, this help began to arrive.

In February 1778, the French and American governments signed a **Treaty of Alliance**. This was a formal agreement to work together. French troops and supplies began to arrive in the United States.

Franklin in France

In 1776, Benjamin Franklin was an American celebrity in France.

Benjamin Franklin

Benjamin Franklin arrived in Paris in December 1776. He was greeted as a great man. Franklin was surrounded, celebrated, and applauded in the streets and theaters. Pictures of him appeared on clocks and rings and walking sticks. Everyone wanted his portrait.

Franklin had an important job to do in France. Once the United States declared independence, the new nation was suddenly at war with Great Britain. Britain had the strongest navy and one of the most powerful armies in the world. The American colonies had neither.

To get help, the Americans turned to France. France was a good choice, because the French hated the British.

The French also saw that America offered opportunities for making plenty of money in trade. There was just one little problem: American values were almost the opposite of French values!

The French had a king, just as the British did. The Americans had just declared that kings were tyrants. The French had aristocrats who believed they were entitled to everything just because they were born into the right family. The Americans believed that all men were created equal.

Paris in the late 1760s

The Granger Collection

To win the war of independence, though, Americans—and Franklin—were willing to set their differences aside. If Franklin could do a good job representing Americans, the French would provide the guns, gunpowder, and other supplies the Americans needed.

Franklin was 70 years old and not exactly handsome, but the French thought he was wonderful. They believed him to be many things he wasn't—and he didn't correct them.

Many French thought that Franklin was a general. But he never fought in a war. They thought he was a farmer, though he'd always lived in cities. He wore a raccoon cap to make himself look like a pioneer, though he had never been interested in traveling into the frontier. The French believed Franklin was a Quaker, though he had never joined a Quaker meeting.

After eight years in France, Franklin achieved his goals. He had been successful in working out treaties that were vital to the future of America. The Treaty of Paris, signed in 1783, was the key to making the United States an independent nation. —*Lisa Jo Rudy*

Northwind Picture Archives

▲ **Franklin was treated like a celebrity in Paris.**

Northwind Picture Archives

▲ **Franklin at the French royal court**

Description Writing Frame

Use the Writing Frame below to orally summarize "Franklin in France."

The French thought Benjamin Franklin had many **interesting characteristics**.

One characteristic was _____,

but _____ .

Another characteristic was _____,

even though _____ .

Franklin even _____
though he had never been interested in traveling into the frontier.

The French also believed _____

_____ .

In fact, Franklin had little interest in religion. Because France

believed **these characteristics**, Franklin _____

_____ .

Use the frame to write the summary on another sheet of paper. Be sure to include the **bold** signal words. Keep this as a model of this Text Structure.

Critical Thinking

1   The Treaty of Alliance was singed by the _____ and American governments.

    A. British

    B. Native American

    C. French

2   Find the word in "The War Begins" that means "a formal meeting."

3   Point to the paragraph in "Franklin in France" that explains why Franklin had an important job to do in France.

4   Review the map on page 151. Were the British and American fortifications far apart? Discuss with a partner.

The scale shows the relationship between distances on a map and real distances.

Digital Learning

For a list of links and activities that relate to this History/Social Science standard, visit the California Treasures Web site at www.macmillanmh.com to access the Content Readers resources. Have children view the Biography "George Washington."

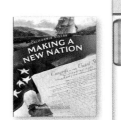

LIFE DURING THE AMERICAN REVOLUTION

American women, rich and poor, young and old, contributed to the struggle for freedom in many ways. Martha Washington, wife of the commander in chief, often visited her husband and his men on the battlefield and helped to nurse the sick and wounded. Back at the Washington's plantation in Mount Vernon, Virginia, Martha helped to keep the farm working. Many other patriot women, such as Sarah Osborn, did the same while their husbands and fathers were off at war.

Some women fought in the Continental army or served as spies. Deborah Sampson and Margaret Corbin disguised themselves as men to join the army. Mary Ludwig Hays McCauley was called Molly Pitcher because she carried pitchers of water to thirsty soldiers during battle. When her husband was wounded during the Battle of Monmouth, she took his place at the cannon. Lydia Darragh and Martha Bell were patriot spies.

Other women wrote books, pamphlets, poems, and letters to inspire Americans to continue to fight. Poet Phillis Wheatley wrote poems of freedom. Mercy Otis Warren wrote a book on the history of the American Revolution. Abigail Adams wrote her husband, political leader John Adams, many letters offering advice. She also formed a committee to help raise money to support soldiers in the Continental army.

Molly Pitcher loaded the cannon during the Battle of Monmouth, New Jersey.

During the war the American people faced constant shortages of food, clothing, and other goods. Manufactured products, such as cloth, kettles, and tools, which had always been imported from Great Britain, were in short supply.

Other shortages were caused by **hoarding**, or hiding away, important goods. Such goods included flour and molasses as well as cotton cloth, clothing, and certain household tools. Some businesses and farmers began **profiteering**, or raising prices, on goods. Laws were passed against profiteering. However, the laws were difficult to enforce, and wartime costs of many products rose sharply.

To pay for the more expensive supplies, Congress began to print more and more paper money. These paper bills were called Continentals. So many Continentals were printed that they soon began to lose value.

The drop in the value of Continentals led to **inflation**. Inflation is a large and rapid rise in prices. For example, a musket that cost five Continentals when it was ordered cost 12 Continentals by the time it was delivered. By the end of the war, a pair of shoes cost 5,000 Continental dollars. People began using the phrase *not worth a Continental* to describe anything that was worthless.

▲ Continental dollars ended up being less valuable than gold and silver coins.

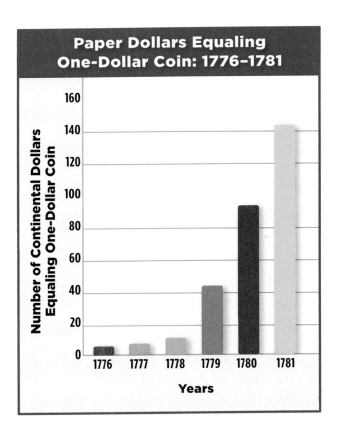

Paper Dollars Equaling One-Dollar Coin: 1776–1781

Number of Continental Dollars Equaling One-Dollar Coin (vertical axis, scale 0–160)

Years (horizontal axis): 1776, 1777, 1778, 1779, 1780, 1781

Martha Washington,
America's *First* First Lady

▲ **Martha Dandridge**

Martha Washington did not stay home when her husband went to war and was not pleased when he became the first President of the United States.

Martha Dandridge was born on June 2, 1731, in New Kent County, Virginia. She was the oldest daughter of a wealthy plantation owner. Martha didn't have great ambitions. She certainly didn't plan to be a famous part of a new nation. By the time she died, though, Martha Dandridge Washington had become a permanent part of American history.

Martha Marries

Martha married at the age of 18. Her first husband was a wealthy older man named Daniel Custis. Like her father, Martha's new husband was a planter. Martha had four children with Custis, but only two survived to grow up. When Daniel Custis died, Martha was still a young woman. She was also very wealthy.

▲ **Martha and George Washington, with two of her children**

Martha married Colonel George Washington on January 6, 1759. George was a colonel in the British army. But the British announced that American army officers could not become full commanders. So George left the army and, with Martha and her children, went to his estate at Mount Vernon in Virginia. Life was comfortable at Mount Vernon, and the couple cared for their children and grandchildren there.

Washington's Mount Vernon estate as it looks today

James P. Blair/Corbis

Martha at War

Even when George Washington became a delegate to the Second Continental Congress, Martha preferred to stay at home in Virginia. She did, however, join her husband from time to time in Philadelphia and even on the battlefield during the American Revolution. She spent the winter of 1775 with her husband's command in Cambridge, Massachusetts. In the spring, she went with George to New York.

After the United States declared independence from England, George Washington became Commander in Chief. Martha went with George to Valley Forge and stayed there all through the cold, harsh winter. She helped the troops to remain positive and prepare for the battles to come. Later, Martha stayed with the army during campaigns in New Jersey, New York, Pennsylvania, and Maryland.

Martha in the White House

When the war was over, George was elected President of the United States. Martha didn't like the idea and wouldn't even go to her husband's inauguration. Once George was President, though, Martha did a good job as official state hostess. The title first lady had not yet been invented. But Martha did a wonderful job creating the role. —*Lisa Jo Rudy*

▼ **General and Mrs. Washington visit the troops.**

Bettmann/Corbis

▼ **The first First Lady holds a reception.**

Brooklyn Museum/Corbis

Cause/Effect Writing Frame

**Use the Writing Frame below to orally summarize
"Life During the American Revolution."**

The Revolution had an **effect** on the daily life of the
American people.

One effect of the revolution was that the people faced constant

shortages of _____ .

The short supply **was caused by** _____

_____ .

Other shortages **were caused by** _____

such as _____ .

Because of hoarding, _____

_____ .

To pay for more expensive supplies _____

_____ .

So many Continentals were printed that it caused _____

_____ . **The result was** inflation.

Use the frame to write the summary on another sheet of paper.
Be sure to include the **bold** signal words. Keep this as a model of
this Text Structure.

Critical Thinking

1 _____ is a large and rapid increase in prices.

    A. Profiteering

    B. Hoarding

    C. Inflation

2 Point to the sentence in "Life During the American Revolution" that explains how Molly Pitcher received her name.

3 Did Martha Washington like the idea of her husband becoming President? Locate the paragraph in "Martha Washington, America's *First* First Lady" that answers the question.

4 Review the photos of Martha Washington on page 159. Discuss with a partner how the pictures support the text.

Photographs and captions give examples that help explain what the text states.

Digital Learning

For a list of links and activities that relate to this History/Social Science standard, visit the California Treasures Web site at www.macmillanmh.com to access the Content Readers resources. Have children view the video "The Struggle for North America."

PLANNING A NEW GOVERNMENT

In 1777 the Congress approved the **Articles of Confederation**. It established the first government of the United States. Under the Articles of Confederation, each state made its own laws, collected its own taxes, and printed its own money. This left the central government weak and caused many problems. In 1786, Daniel Shays, a farmer in Massachusetts, organized thousands of farmers to protest against taxes. Many of the farmers were veterans of the American Revolution, who were owed money from Congress and could not pay their taxes. A bloody battle, known as **Shays's Rebellion**, followed. Troops were called out to put down the rebellion, and eight men died.

On May 25, 1778, **delegates** representing 12 states met at a convention in Philadelphia. A delegate is a person chosen to speak or act for other people. Only Rhode Island did not send any delegates. Its residents feared that the convention would weaken the power of the small states.

Most of the delegates expected to fix the Articles of Confederation. James Madison believed that this could not be done. He arrived in Philadelphia with a plan for a strong national government, called the **Virginia Plan**. Madison convinced most of the delegates to vote against fixing up the Articles of Confederation. Instead, they began work on a new plan of government. The meeting in Philadelphia then became known as the Constitutional Convention because it worked to produce a constitution for a new national government.

The argument over representation lasted for a month. Finally Roger Sherman, a delegate from Connecticut, proposed a compromise. Sherman suggested the legislature be broken into two parts. In the **House of Representatives**, each state would be represented according to its populations. States with more people would receive more voting power. In the **Senate**, however, each state, no matter what its size, would have two votes. Members of the House of Representatives would serve two years and be chosen directly by the people. Members of the Senate would serve six-year terms and be chosen by state legislatures.

▼ **John Hancock was the governor of Massachusetts during Shays's Rebellion.**

Sherman's proposal, adopted on July 16, 1787, became known as the **Great Compromise**. To make a law, both the Senate and the House of Representatives would have to approve it. This concept was closer to the New Jersey plan, and it was a victory for the less populated states.

Delegates wanted the United States to have a President but feared that people might not choose a good candidate. Had Congress picked the President as Madison suggested, the President would not be independent. The delegates compromised by creating the **Electoral College**. In the Electoral College, each state has a certain number of electoral votes based on the number of representatives it has in Congress. A candidate must win a majority of the electoral votes to become President.

More than one third of the delegates in the convention were plantation owners with enslaved workers. Some delegates did not want enslaved people to be counted as part of the population. However, John Rutledge of South Carolina threatened that the Southern states would refuse to join any country that gave Congress the power to prevent the slave trade.

In the end, a compromise was reached. Every five enslaved people in a state would count as three free people for representation of the state in Congress. The delegates also agreed to end slave trading with other countries in 1808.

On September 17, 1787, 39 delegates signed the Constitution. It had been a difficult struggle to reach an agreement.

When the Convention finished its work, Eliza Powell of Philadelphia asked Benjamin Franklin what kind of government the delegates had prepared. Franklin answered, "A republic, if you can keep it." The hard job of keeping the republic alive still lay ahead, and it continues to this day.

▼ **This painting of the signing of the Constitution is in the Capitol Building in Washington, D.C.**

How Free Are We to Speak Freely?

Alex Wong/Getty Images

The First Amendment guarantees Americans the right to free speech, but what that means is still being debated.

Karen Bleier/AFP/Getty Images

▲ **Americans have the right to speak out against or in favor of government polices.**

Americans treasure free speech and expression. Our right to share our ideas—by writing them in books, shouting them at a rally, or ironing them onto T-shirts—is protected by the First Amendment. The amendment is one of ten in the Bill of Rights, added to the Constitution in 1791.

The First Amendment is often amended. Court decisions have limited its freedoms to protect national security or the privacy of individuals, among other goals. But speaking out is one of the fundamental rights—and responsibilities—of every American. This includes speaking out about the government's policies, whether for them or against them.

The First Amendment

"Congress shall make no law respecting an establishment of religion, or prohibiting the free exercise thereof; or abridging the freedom of speech; or the right of the people peaceably to assemble, and to petition the government for a redress of grievances. . ."

Our right to free speech is guaranteed in the Bill of Rights. ▶

NARA

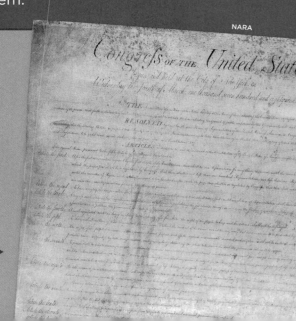

Free Speech or Illegal Speech?

In addition to spoken words, the First Amendment protects written words. A very important part of that protection is freedom of the press. American journalists—whether writing for a newspaper, a magazine, or a Web site—write about almost anything they think is important.

Still, there are certain types of free speech that are never allowed. Some of these include

○ **Treason.** Giving away U.S. secrets to the enemy is a crime, and can be punished very severely.

○ **Slander.** Saying untrue, negative things about another person in a public way is against the law.

○ **Obscenity.** Obscene words and pictures are illegal—though the definition of obscenity has changed a great deal over the years.

Tricky Questions About Freedom of Speech

Is burning the American flag protected by the First Amendment? Is wearing a T-shirt expressing an unpopular opinion protected? Do people who are under age 21 have the same free speech rights as people 21 and older? Are students on the grounds of public schools guaranteed the right of free speech?

Evan Vucci/AP Photo

▲ **How free are students to speak freely?**

In 2007 the Supreme Court decided a case in which a student had been suspended for holding up a sign outside a school. The sign said nothing illegal, but the school felt that its content was unacceptable. The court ruled that the school was right, but also added "while the court has limited student free speech rights in the past, young people do not give up all their First Amendment rights when they enter a school." How far do students' free speech rights go? The Supreme Court will continue to answer this question as time goes on. —*Martha Pickerill and Susan Moger*

Description Writing Frame

Use the Writing Frame below to orally summarize "How Free Are We to Speak Freely?"

The First Amendment guarantees Americans the right to free speech.

For example, we can share our ideas by _____

_____.

This includes _____
whether for them or against them.

An important part of the First Amendment is _____

_____.

For example, American journalists can _____

_____.

Still, there are certain types of free speech that are never allowed,

such as _____.

The _____
decides the difference between free speech and a criminal act.

Use the frame to write the summary on another sheet of paper.
Be sure to include the **bold** signal words. Keep this as a model of
this Text Structure.

Critical Thinking

1 In the _____, each state has two votes.

    A. House of Representatives

    B. Senate

    C. Convention

2 Point to the sentence in "Planning a New Government" that defines the word *delegate*.

3 Locate the paragraph in "How Free Are We to Speak Freely?" that explains how the First Amendment is often amended.

4 Orally create your own caption for your favorite photograph in "Planning a New Government."

> Captions give the reader additional information about the subject of an article.

Digital Learning

For a list of links and activities that relate to this History/Social Science standard, visit the California Treasures Web site at www.macmillanmh.com to access the Content Readers resources. Have children view the video "A New Nation."

MOVING WEST

The American Revolution had created a new nation, but there were still many Americans without land. About one in five Americans lived in **poverty**. Poverty means people living without enough money for proper food or supplies. Without land, people's lives were unlikely to improve.

Between 1790 and 1820 the population of the United States grew, from about 4 million to nearly 10 million. Most Americans were farmers. They needed large families to do the many chores a farm required. When farmers died, their land was divided among their children. Even a large farm might not provide enough land for all of the children.

In the mid-1800s the population of the United States began to change dramatically. In addition to the growing number of free blacks and enslaved African Americans, between 1845 and 1860 more immigrants came to the United States than ever before.

Many Europeans came to find work. A million Irish people immigrated to the United States to escape starvation. Some Chinese came in the 1840s to seek fortunes. Later they worked on the railroads.

Some people moved to cities, but others looked to the open lands in the West. For poor people, these lands offered a chance to build a new life.

Westward expansion was possible due to the new routes to travel. In 1769 a trader named John Findley chose an experienced explorer, Daniel Boone, to help him find an inland trail from North Carolina to Kentucky. They found a natural passage through the Appalachian Mountains, which they called the Cumberland Gap. A road was built through the gap. Boone and Findley's Wilderness Road became the main route for Americans heading west.

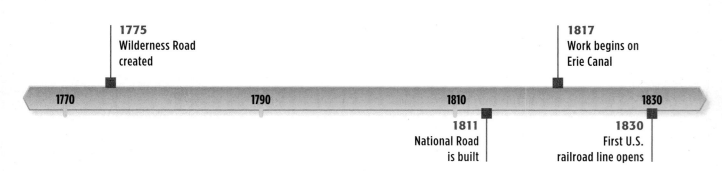

1775
Wilderness Road created

1817
Work begins on Erie Canal

1770   1790   1810   1830

1811
National Road is built

1830
First U.S. railroad line opens

In the early 1800s most people traveled in **stagecoaches**, which were large, horse-drawn carriages. Most roads were narrow dirt trails dotted with potholes and tree stumps. When it rained, the roads became muddy messes. Even on a good day, travel on these roads was slow.

In 1811 the federal government built the National Road from Cumberland, Maryland, to Vandalia, Illinois. It was America's first interstate highway. This stone and gravel road linked the East with what was then the western frontier.

Transportation improved even more after the invention of the **steam engine**. A steam engine uses compressed steam to power its motor. It can produce much greater power than a team of horses, so it can pull heavier loads.

An American inventor and painter named Robert Fulton thought that a steam engine could be used to power a boat upstream. Fulton worked for years on his design. In August 1807, Fulton's steamboat, the Clermont, was ready to run up the Hudson River from New York City to Albany. Some people made fun of the boat, because they did not believe it would work. However, the 150-mile trip took just 32 hours. Other boats took from 8 to 11 days for the same trip.

By 1855 more than 700 steamboats carried people and goods on rivers around the United States. Migration from the eastern United States to the West increased as a result.

People had traveled by railroad for years, but on early railroads, horses pulled coaches over iron rails. In 1814 British inventor George Stephenson built the first train with a steam engine inside. These new trains were nicknamed the iron horses.

In 1830, Peter Cooper, an American merchant, built a small locomotive named Tom Thumb. At first, few people believed the Tom Thumb could move. A Baltimore stagecoach company challenged Cooper and his locomotive to a race against a horse-drawn carriage. The little train lost the race, but railroads soon became the main form of transportation in the nation.

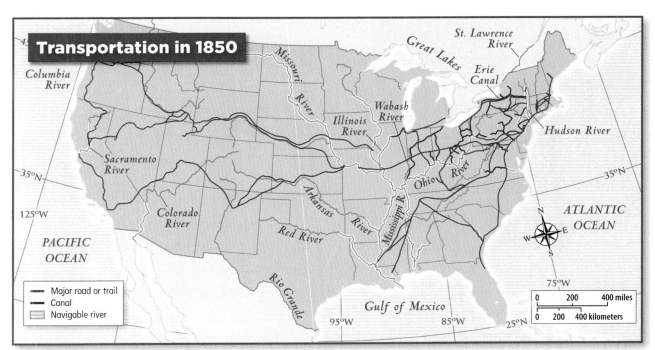

Transportation in 1850

Columbia River
Missouri River
Great Lakes
St. Lawrence River
Erie Canal
Wabash River
Illinois River
Hudson River
Sacramento River
Arkansas River
Ohio River
ATLANTIC OCEAN
35°N
125°W
Colorado River
Red River
Mississippi R.
PACIFIC OCEAN
Rio Grande
Gulf of Mexico
95°W
85°W
25°N
75°W

— Major road or trail
— Canal
▢ Navigable river

0   200   400 miles
0   200   400 kilometers

America in 1850

The midpoint of the 19th century was a challenging time for the United States.

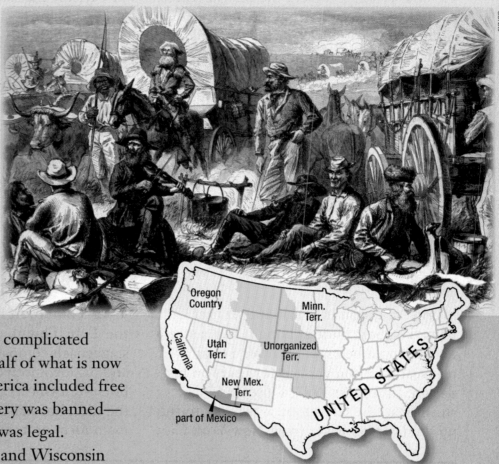

Corbis

Pioneers headed west during the 1850s. ▶

America in 1850 was a complicated place. The eastern half of what is now the United States of America included free states—states where slavery was banned— and states where slavery was legal. Everything west of Iowa and Wisconsin was a territory and not yet included in the United States. Zachary Taylor was President.

In New England, writers were producing newspapers and literature. The *New York Times* newspaper was founded. Nathaniel Hawthorne's *The Scarlet Letter* was published.

In the Midwest, Kansas City was founded. Pioneering farmers still faced land disputes with Native Americans. New treaties clarified who owned which land.

▲ **States and territories, 1850**

Brigham Young, the founder of the Church of the Latter Day Saints (Mormons), had led his followers to Salt Lake City. There in the Utah territory the Mormons began to build their home.

In the West, the Gold Rush had brought thousands of people to California. Thousands more were moving to the Pacific Northwest from Missouri along the Oregon Trail. Pioneers were making their way to the Pacific coast, and the population was exploding.

What About Slavery?

Opinions about slavery were mixed in the United States in 1850. In the South, there was a strong belief that slaves were important to the growth of the nation. In the North, there were abolitionists who believed slavery was wrong and should be banned throughout the U.S.

California had petitioned to become a state. But should it be a free state or a slave state? The Congress was divided, concerned about upsetting a balance between free and slave states. Senator Henry Clay of Kentucky offered a compromise. He suggested that California be admitted as a free state. Meanwhile, new territories called New Mexico, Nevada, Arizona, and Utah would be neither free nor slave territories.

The Granger Collection

▲ **Henry Clay argues for the California Compromise**

To get support from slave states, Clay proposed a new law. The law required citizens to assist in capturing fugitive slaves, and it denied runaway slaves the right to a trial by jury. Clay's compromise, called the Compromise of 1850, was adopted. California entered the Union as a free state, but slaves were subjected to the new Fugitive Slave Act. In the end, this harsh law inspired abolitionists to fight even harder to outlaw slavery throughout the United States—something that finally happened 1865 with passage of the Thirteenth Amendment to the Constitution.

People of the United States— 1850 and Today

There are 11 times more people in the United States today than there were in 1850. But about the same percentage of people were born here as were born abroad.

In 1850, more than 90 percent of immigrants came from Europe. Today only 23 percent of immigrants come from Europe. Instead, the majority come from Latin America and Asia. —*Lisa Jo Rudy*

In the News in 1850

- The women's suffrage movement got started. Women started campaigning for the right to vote.
- I. M. Singer and Company patented the first sewing machine.
- P. T. Barnum brought singer Jenny Lind, the Swedish Nightingale, to America. He advertised everywhere. She was met at the dock by 30,000 New Yorkers!
- Joel Houghton invented the first automatic dishwasher.
- Levi Strauss began making blue jeans.

The Granger Collection

171

Sequence Writing Frame

Use the Writing Frame below to orally summarize "Moving West."

By 1820 _____

_____ .

Most Americans _____ and needed _____

_____ .

In the mid-1800s _____

_____ .

There were a growing number of _____ .

In the 1840s some _____ .

They also _____ .

Then many _____ .

A million Irish people _____ .

By 1860 _____

_____ .

Use the frame to write the summary on another sheet of paper.
Be sure to include the **bold** signal words. Keep this as a model of
this Text Structure.

Critical Thinking

1. In the early 1800s most people traveled by _____.

    A. stagecoach

    B. steamboat

    C. railroad

2. Find the sentence in "Moving West" that explains the importance of the steam engine.

3. Find the paragraph in "America in 1850" that describes the reason for the Fugitive Slave Act.

4. Does the time line on page 168 provide any information that is not in the text? Discuss with a partner.

> A time line is a quick way to present a lot of information.

Digital Learning

For a list of links and activities that relate to this History/Social Science standard, visit the California Treasures Web site at www.macmillanmh.com to access the Content Readers resources. Have children view the video "The Nation Expands."

THE LOUISIANA PURCHASE

President Thomas Jefferson favored expanding the United State farther west to make more land available for farmers. He was also especially worried about New Orleans. If this city was controlled by another county, New Orleans and the Mississippi River could be closed to American trade.

In 1803 New Orleans and the lands west of the Mississippi River formed a French colony called Louisiana. This huge area stretched from the Mississippi River to the Rocky Mountains and from the Gulf of Mexico to the Canadian border.

The United States was able to purchase nearly 530 million acres of North America for $15 million, or about $200 million in current dollars. This came out to about 3.5 cents an acre. **The Louisiana Purchase** doubled the size of the United States.

The Louisiana Territory stretched so far west that some Americans were not sure what they had purchased. Jefferson organized expeditions to explore the area.

Jefferson selected Meriwether Lewis, his personal secretary, to lead the expedition. In June 1803 Lewis offered to share command with William Clark, a brother of George Rodgers Clark, the Revolutionary War leader.

▼ **Meriwether Lewis (top) and William Clark (bottom) kept careful journals of the plants and animals they studied on their journey west.**

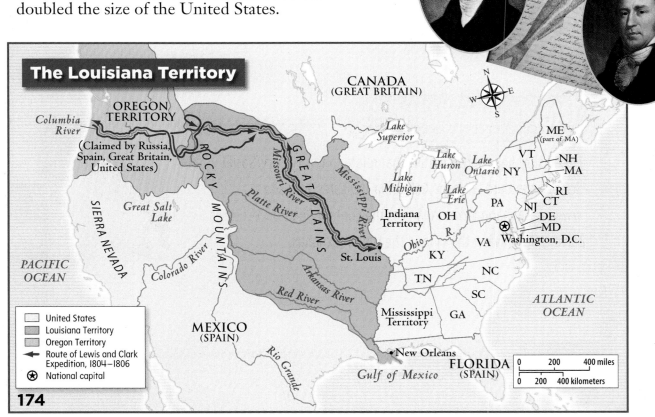

The Louisiana Territory

174

In May of 1804 the Lewis and Clark Expedition headed west from St. Louis, on the Mississippi River. In 1805 they were joined by a guide and interpreter, a Shoshone woman named Sacagawea. Led by Native American guides, the expedition traveled 8,000 miles. The travelers crossed the Rocky Mountains and followed the Columbia River to the Pacific Ocean. They did not return to St. Louis until 1806.

Jefferson also organized other expeditions for exploring the new territories. In 1805 Zebulon Pike led an expedition to search for the source, or beginning, of the Mississippi River. He did not find the river's source, but Pike's expedition did establish an American presence in the Louisiana Territory.

In another expedition, Pike reached the Rocky Mountains, in the Oregon Territory. There he tried unsuccessfully to climb the mountain that is now named after him.

The Oregon Territory included most of the Pacific Northwest. It contained what are now Washington, Oregon, northern Idaho, part of Montana, and the Canadian province of British Columbia.

The Oregon Territory did not attract settlers until the late 1830s. The first Americans in the area were missionaries who tried to convert Native Americans to Christianity. They sent letters back east describing the rich farmland of the Willamette Valley in Oregon. Midwestern farm families began catching Oregon Fever—the desire to get a fresh start in the West. Between 1841 and 1845 the American population of Oregon increased from 400 to 6,000.

People moving to Oregon traveled on the Oregon Trail. This wagon route connected Missouri to western Oregon. The first settlers appeared on the Oregon Trail in 1841. By 1860 more than 300,000 people had traveled on it to the West.

The covered wagon that the settlers took west was known as a Prairie Schooner. It was lighter and smaller than the Conestoga wagon of earlier times. Each Prairie Schooner could carry everything a family would need, not only for their journey but also to set up houses when they arrived. The wagons carried flour, water, dried meat, farm tools, seeds, weapons, clothing, books, medicine, spare wagon parts, pans, and nails.

It took about six months to travel the 2,000-mile route west. Most settlers joined a wagon train. One wagon train could include hundreds of wagons. It offered protection and help in times of trouble.

Everyone had a daily task on the trail. Men drove the wagons and repaired the equipment. Women cooked, set up tents, and washed clothes. Children hunted for buffalo chips, which were used as fuel for fires. One settler remembered, "Those who crossed the plains . . . never forgot the . . . thirst, the intense heat and bitter cold, the craving hunger, and the utter physical exhaustion of the trial."

A HISTORIC JOURNEY

Lewis and Clark's big adventure began more than 200 years ago.

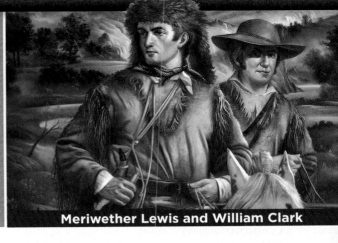
David Bowers

Meriwether Lewis and William Clark

On January 18, 1803, President Thomas Jefferson asked Congress to approve a daring mission. He wanted to send a team of explorers from the Mississippi River to the Pacific Ocean for the first time. The cost to taxpayers would be $2,500.

Congress agreed, and by the following year Meriwether Lewis and William Clark were on their way. The two old Army buddies were leading a 33-member Corps of Discovery.

Why Go West?

In 1803 the land west of the Mississippi was known only to dozens of tribes of American Indians and some Europeans who worked along the Missouri River.

Jefferson hoped that the expedition would find a Northwest Passage, another river that would lead straight to the Pacific Ocean. He also wanted to improve relations with the Indians.

The urge to explore the West was driven by another big event in 1803. That was the Louisiana Purchase. Jefferson agreed to pay France $15 million for a huge chunk of western land. He was eager to explore this land.

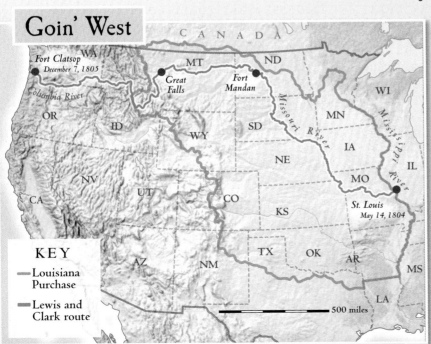

Goin' West

CANADA

Fort Clatsop
December 7, 1805

WA

MT

ND

Great Falls

Fort Mandan

WI

Columbia River

OR

ID

SD

MN

Missouri River

WY

NE

IA

Mississippi River

IL

NV

UT

CO

MO

St. Louis
May 14, 1804

CA

KS

AR

TX

OK

MS

AZ

NM

LA

KEY
— Louisiana Purchase
— Lewis and Clark route

500 miles

Blazing the Trail

Lewis, 29, was Jefferson's neighbor and had been his secretary. After the President asked him to lead the mission, Lewis got William Clark, 33, to join him on the trip.

The explorers and their crew kept journals during the trip. The journals are filled with misspelled words. Lewis wrote of the "beatifull" plains. Clark told of being bitten by pesky "musquetors." He also described the power of seeing the Pacific for the first time: "Ocian in view! O! the joy."

Surprises Along the Way

There were misunderstandings between the explorers and Indians. But there was only one violent conflict. In fact, a Shoshone guide was a vital member of the crew. Her name was Sacagawea (sac•uh•juh•WEE•uh).

Sacagawea guided the crew through Indian territory to the Pacific. Then she guided them back.

Of course, the United States later fought the Indians and took their land. "[The expedition] has that mixed quality of great news for one people and bad news for another," Patricia Limerick says. She is with the Center of the American West at the University of Colorado in Boulder.

While scouting, Lewis realized that there is no Northwest Passage to the Pacific Ocean. To reach the coast, the explorers had to hike over mountains. They had to haul boats over land. But despite the lack of a Northwest Passage, generations of Americans have declared the mission a success. —*Martha Pickerill*

▼ **A page from Clark's journal**

Charles Rex Arbogast/AP Photo

▼ **Sacagawea points the way as the expedition pushes west.**

Corbis/Bettmann

▼ **Clark's compass**

American Museum of Natural History

Problem/Solution Writing Frame

Use the Writing Frame below to orally summarize "A Historic Journey."

President Thomas Jefferson had a **problem**. He wanted to find _____

_____ .

He also wanted to _____

_____ .

To solve this problem, Jefferson _____

_____ .

Lewis and Clark kept journals on the trip. While scouting, Lewis

realized _____

_____ .

To solve this problem, the explorers _____

and _____ .

But despite the lack of a Northwest Passage, generations of Americans have declared the mission a success.

Use the frame to write the summary on another sheet of paper. Be sure to include the **bold** signal words. Keep this as a model of this Text Structure.

Critical Thinking

1 The Louisiana Purchase _____ the size of the United States.

   A. quadrupled

   B. doubled

   C. tripled

2 Find the sentence in "The Louisiana Purchase" that names the present-day areas that were part of the Oregon Territory.

3 Locate the paragraph in "A Historic Journey" that explains contact between the explorers and Indians.

4 Look at the map on page 176. With a partner, discuss Lewis and Clark's route.

The legend or key helps you understand the symbols on a map.

Digital Learning

For a list of links and activities that relate to this History/Social Science standard, visit the California Treasures Web site at www.macmillanmh.com to access the Content Readers resources. Have children view the Biography "Sacagawea."

THE UNITED STATES EXPANDS

After the Civil War the United States gained the territories of **Alaska** and **Hawaii**. For the first time the United States acquired land beyond its borders. Soon other territories would follow.

Russia had colonized Alaska in the eighteenth century. It was a vast land of more than 500,000 square miles. Its people, especially the Inuit, have lived there for thousands of years. In 1867, Russia offered to sell its colony to the United States. Secretary of State William Seward said the U.S. government would pay $7.2 million for Alaska, or about 2 cents an acre. Some Americans thought the deal was foolish and referred to Alaska as Seward's ice box or Seward's folly.

How wrong they were quickly became apparent. In the 1880s gold was discovered in the area that is now Juneau, Alaska's state capital. Alaska's plentiful resources also included fish, lumber, and oil.

The United States gained Hawaii in a different way. The Pacific islands of Hawaii have been inhabited since the first people reached them between A.D. 600 and A.D. 1000. In 1778 an English sea captain named James Cook landed in Hawaii and opened the way for Christian missionaries, who arrived there in the late 1820s.

By the 1890s Americans had migrated there. Some had become wealthy by building large pineapple and sugarcane plantations. **Queen Liliuokalani** (lee•lee•oo•who•kah•LAH•nee), Hawaii's ruler, wanted to restore power to native-born Hawaiians. In 1893 the American planters revolted and overthrew the queen. Then they asked that Hawaii join the United States. At first, President Grover Cleveland refused, but in 1898 Hawaii became a U.S. possession.

In 1959 Alaska became the forty-ninth state, and Hawaii became the fiftieth.

In the **Spanish-American War** of 1898, the United States gained the islands of Puerto Rico, Guam, and the Philippines.

Philippine rebels had been battling the Spanish when the United States took control of the Philippines. Under Emilio Aguinaldo (ah•gwee•NAHL•doh),

Filipinos fought for independence until 1901. In 1946 the Philippines gained independence. However, both Guam and Puerto Rico have chosen to remain part of the United States, and their people are U.S. citizens.

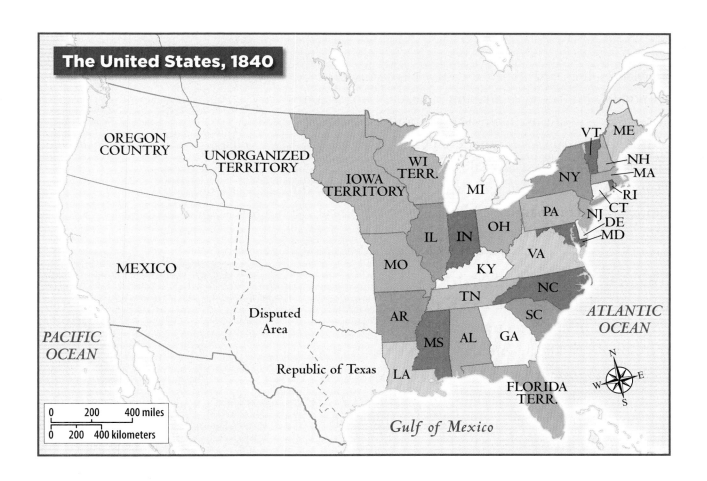

The United States, 1840

OREGON COUNTRY

UNORGANIZED TERRITORY

IOWA TERRITORY

WI TERR.

MI

MEXICO

IL

IN

OH

PA

MO

KY

VA

Disputed Area

AR

TN

NC

Republic of Texas

MS

AL

GA

SC

NY

VT

ME

NH

MA

RI

CT

NJ

DE

MD

ATLANTIC OCEAN

LA

FLORIDA TERR.

PACIFIC OCEAN

Gulf of Mexico

0   200   400 miles
0   200   400 kilometers

N E W S

Some State Capital Snapshots

The cities that serve as state capitals are as different and as interesting as the states and regions they represent.

Montpelier, Vermont

Tiny Montpelier, Vermont, is the smallest state capital in the United States. With only about 8,000 residents, it seems too small to be important. Its state capitol building, though, is just as impressive as that of any other state.

Montpelier is in a beautiful spot in the Green Mountains. In town are farmers' markets, shops, and historic sites—but not a single fast-food restaurant! Although Montpelier is nowhere near the sea, three U.S. Navy ships have carried the name U.S.S. *Montpelier*. Why? Montpelier was the birthplace of one of the most famous navy commanders in U.S. history, Admiral George Dewey.

Joseph Sohm/Visions of America/Corbis

▲ Vermont's impressive capitol building

Sacramento, California

In 1848, John Sutter discovered gold near a sawmill on his land in north central California. In 1849, the Gold Rush began, and the tiny settlement of Sacramento soon became a boomtown. Even after the Gold Rush ended, Sacramento continued to grow and thrive. Soon it was a stop for the Pony Express and the Central Pacific Railroad.

Today there are about 450,000 people living in Sacramento, and more than 2 million in the metropolitan area. One of the city's most famous landmarks is the Tower Bridge connecting Sacramento and West Sacramento.

Gerald French/Corbis

▲ Sacramento's Tower Bridge

Denver, Colorado

Denver is nicknamed the Mile-High City because it is exactly 5,280 feet above sea level! It's also the biggest town in Colorado. Like Sacramento, Denver was founded as the result of a gold rush. In this case, it was the Pike's Peak Gold Rush, which started in 1858. Today Denver is home to more than a half million people.

Denver gets an average of 300 days a year of sunshine. Another cool Denver fact is that the roof of the Denver airport was designed to look like the Rocky Mountains.

Bill Ross/Corbis

▲ Denver's skyline against the Rocky Mountains

Springfield, Illinois

Springfield is best known as the birthplace of Abraham Lincoln. A big new Lincoln museum in Springfield tells the story of Lincoln's life and work.

Springfield is actually the third city to serve as the capital of Illinois. The first capital was Kaskaskia. Then Vandalia became the capital. Finally, a group of legislators called the Long Nine succeeded in getting the capitol moved to Springfield in 1839. The Long Nine got their name because all of them, including Lincoln, were over six feet tall!

Jason Reed/Corbis

▲ Springfield's Abraham Lincoln Presidential Library and Museum

Columbia, South Carolina

Columbia, South Carolina, was founded in 1806 and named for Christopher Columbus. It was a planned city, laid out in 400 blocks along the Congaree river. The blocks were divided into half-acre lots. Buyers had to build a house at least 30 feet long and 18 feet wide within three years or pay a fine.

The city's planners also made sure that all the streets were at least 100 feet wide. That's because they believed that mosquitoes, which are common in the area, couldn't fly more than 60 feet without dying of starvation!

Mary Ann Chastain/AP Photo

▲ Columbia's African American History Monument

Compare/Contrast Writing Frame

Use the Writing Frame below to orally summarize "The United States Expands."

Alaska and Hawaii are **similar** in many ways. After the Civil War,

they were **both** _____

by the United States. They are **also alike because** in 1959 _____

_____ .

In some ways, however, _____ and _____

_____ **are different**.

In 1867, William Seward _____ .

In comparison, in 1893 in Hawaii _____

_____ . In 1898 _____

_____ .

So _____ and _____

are alike in some ways and **different** in others.

Use the frame to write the summary on another sheet of paper. Be sure to include the **bold** signal words. Keep this as a model of this Text Structure.

Critical Thinking

1. Puerto Rico and _____ have chosen to remain territories of the United States.

   A. Guam

   B. Philippines

   C. Hawaii

2. Find the sentence in "The United States Expands" that names the last Queen of Hawaii.

3. Find the paragraph in "Some State Capital Snapshots" that describes the Mile-High City.

4. Study the map on page 181 with a partner. Discuss how the United States has changed since 1840.

On maps, borders between states usually are drawn differently from the border between nations.

Digital Learning

For a list of links and activities that relate to this History/Social Science standard, visit the California Treasures Web site at www.macmillanmh.com to access the Content Readers resources. Have children view the video "The Nation Expands."

Illustration Acknowledgements

12, 24: Jeff Grunewald. 37: Linda Nye. 42: Bart Vallecoccia. 43: Laurie O' Keefe. 54: (bl) John Edwards. 55, 60, 72, 79, John Kauffman. 91: Jeff Grunewald

Photography Acknowledgements

All photos for Macmillan/McGraw-Hill except as noted below:

Cover: Alamy. 19: Oak Ridge National Laboratory. 25: Steve Raymer/National Geographic Image Collection/Getty Images. 30: Jim Zuckerman/CORBIS. 31: (tcl) Clouds Hill Imaging Ltd./CORBIS; (bcr) Michael Gabridge/Visuals Unlimited. 61: (tc) Lawrence Migdale/Photo Researchers. 85: NASA. 90: NASA/CORBIS. 102: Nationalmuseet Copenhagen Denmark/Dagli Orti (A)/The Art Archive. 114: North Wind Picture Archives. 118: North Wind Picture Archives. 121: The Granger Collection, New York. 126: Grant Heilman/Grant Heilman Photography. 133: North Wind Picture Archives. 139: The Granger Collection, New York. 144: The Granger Collection, New York. 145: Réunion des Musées Nationaux/Art Resource, NY. 156: The Granger Collection, New York. 157: (tr) The Granger Collection, New York; (t) The Granger Collection, New York. 162: (br) Bettmann/CORBIS; (b) The Granger Collection, New York. 174: (l to r) The Granger Collection, New York; National Historical Park, Independence, Missouri, MO, USA/Bridgeman Art Library; The Granger Collection, New York